Prompted

PROMPTED is a clear and practical guide that makes AI interaction accessible to a wide audience. It fills the gap between dense technical manuals and overly simplistic guides by offering actionable frameworks and techniques to help readers use AI as a tool for creativity, collaboration, and productivity. The book shifts the focus from coding or quick tips to teaching readers how to think with AI as a strategic partner. It emphasizes building lasting skills that grow with the technology, giving readers the tools to navigate and shape the evolving AI landscape.

Key themes include human-AI collaboration, the ethical responsibilities of prompting, and the creative opportunities that emerge from effective AI communication. This book stands out by addressing the urgent need for approachable, practical knowledge as AI becomes central to work and innovation. It will empower professionals across industries to unlock AI's potential while staying mindful of ethical and practical considerations.

Antti Innanen is the CEO of Dot, a legal design consultancy, and LEGIT, an AI consultancy. He specializes in making complex systems more human-centered and is at the forefront of applying AI in professional services. He frequently writes about AI, legal design, and the future of work.

Prompted

How to Create and Communicate with AI

Antti Innanen

CRC Press
Taylor & Francis Group
Boca Raton London New York

CRC Press is an imprint of the
Taylor & Francis Group, an **informa** business

First edition published 2026
by CRC Press
2385 NW Executive Center Drive, Suite 320, Boca Raton FL 33431
and by CRC Press
4 Park Square, Milton Park, Abingdon, Oxon, OX14 4RN
CRC Press is an imprint of Taylor & Francis Group, LLC

ISBN: 9781041066637 (hbk)
ISBN: 9781041066613 (pbk)
ISBN: 9781003636502 (ebk)

DOI: 10.1201/9781003636502

Typeset in Oro
by KnowledgeWorks Global Ltd.

Contents

Introduction

You're about to learn the most important skill of the AI era: the art of conversation with artificial minds. Not coding. Not data science. Not machine learning theory. But something more fundamental: how to think alongside AI.

The secret to AI isn't better prompts. It's better thinking.

Most people think of AI as a simple question-and-answer machine: ask, and it responds. But with the right prompts, it becomes something far more powerful: a creative partner that challenges your thinking, expands your perspective, and helps you solve problems in ways you never imagined.

Modern AI tools don't just store and retrieve information. They generate ideas, explain complex concepts, and uncover unexpected connections. But they come with clear limitations: they struggle with exact facts, real-time events, and absolute accuracy.

There's a method to getting consistently great results from AI, and it's often transferable across different systems. At its core, ***the art of crafting great prompts is the art of clear thought***.

This book is not just about writing prompts. It is about how we think. It explores different mental models and frameworks from philosophy and psychology, offering new ways to engage with AI.

THE NEW ESSENTIAL SKILLS

AI is becoming an essential skill for professionals in every field. But with new tools constantly emerging, each claiming to revolutionize how we work, how do you keep up?

Prompting manuals from just a year or two ago already feel outdated. AI models have evolved rapidly, and techniques that once seemed cutting-edge are now clunky or irrelevant.

The landscape is shifting too fast for static rulebooks or prompting guidelines. Instead of memorizing rigid formulas, the real skill is learning *how to think* with AI: adapting, experimenting, and developing an intuition for what works.

True AI expertise is not about chasing trends or learning tricks. It is about developing *meta-skills,* timeless abilities that remain valuable no matter how the tools evolve.

To truly master AI, you need four key skills:

1 Understanding AI at a Deeper Level

To work effectively with AI, you need to know how it work, not just how to use it. This means grasping core concepts like biases, hallucinations, and system limitations. By understanding why AI produces certain results, you can use it more confidently and safely.

2 Fundamental Thinking Skills: Mental Models

Thinking *with* AI is a skill of its own. Mental models—structured ways of thinking—help you frame problems, interpret results, and push AI beyond surface-level outputs. The right mental models unlock AI's full potential, leading to deeper insights and better results.

3 Iterative Ways of Working

AI rarely gets things perfect on the first try. The best results come through iteration: testing, refining, and improving AI outputs until they are truly useful. Working with AI is not about passively accepting what it gives you but actively shaping it into something better.

4 Tastemaking: Knowing What's Good

When AI simplifies content creation and decision-making, taste becomes the true differentiator. Whether you are writing, designing, or making strategic choices, your ability to recognize quality and make refined decisions is what sets you apart. But can taste be taught or developed? Absolutely.

I believe these four skills are worth investing in *right now.* They are not tied to any specific tool or technique but will remain valuable long-term, even as prompting evolves into something entirely different from what it is today.

Mastering them will ensure you stay ahead, no matter how AI changes.

HOW THIS BOOK IS STRUCTURED

These four skills are at the heart of mastering AI, but this book is not structured as a step-by-step guide to each one. Instead, it is divided into two parts: **Foundations** and **Practical Applications.**

This is a deliberate choice. A strictly categorized structure would be too rigid, and honestly, a bit boring. **There is a story that builds as the book progresses, starting with communication and moving toward more abstract ideas.** Each chapter goes a little deeper than the one before. The second part of the book shifts toward a more pragmatic focus, exploring how to apply these ideas in practice.

You'll find all of these ideas woven throughout the book. As you read, you start recognizing patterns: *"Oh, this is actually about tastemaking!"* or *"This connects to mental models!"*, and that's exactly the point. At some point, it might all click (cue the *Mind Blown* meme), and you'll see that, in one way or another, everything in this book comes back to these four skills.

The book is also typeset in a way that helps guide you through the material. I wanted the main ideas to pop, so you can catch quick insights as you read and come back to them later when you have more time.

PROMPTING MATTERS

Before we go any further, there is one key principle you need to understand: **the quality of your prompt *directly* impacts the quality of the output.**

Consider the difference between these two prompts:

"Tell me about dogs."

> "Write a 100-word paragraph about how dogs help reduce stress. Include three main benefits, reference recent research, and make it easy to understand."

The first is open-ended and vague, leaving the AI to guess what you want. The second is precise, shaping the AI's response to your specific needs.

The second prompt yields better results because it provides clear direction. This book will teach you how to craft precise prompts, but more importantly, it will help you develop the mental models and thinking patterns that remain valuable even as AI tools evolve.

You might wonder, "*Can't I just type whatever I want and let the AI figure it out?*" But while AI models are becoming increasingly sophisticated, the quality of their responses still heavily depends on the quality of your thinking.

> **As Nvidia CEO Jensen Huang put it: "You can't just randomly ask a bunch of questions."**

Better thinking leads to better prompts, which lead to better answers.

When you learn to think *with* AI, you're learning something more valuable than specific prompting techniques. You're developing meta-skills that help you adapt to and thrive with any AI system you encounter. Most importantly, you learn to guide these tools thoughtfully rather than letting them guide you.

A WORD ON RESPONSIBILITY

AI can make us smarter, faster, and more creative. However, it can also lead us in the wrong direction. Every time you use AI, verify its facts, question its assumptions, and consider who might be affected by your outputs.

This isn't just about avoiding mistakes. AI embeds human biases, can spread misinformation, and affects both privacy and agency in ways we're still discovering. Use it thoughtfully. Stay critical. The examples and techniques in this book are meant to guide you, not to be followed blindly.

> **AI isn't a magic solution to every problem. Sometimes a conversation with a colleague or a quiet moment of reflection is exactly what you need. The goal is to use AI well when it matters most.**

As we explore these tools together, we'll focus on understanding both their potential and their limits. With careful and informed use, we can shape AI's role in ways that benefit everyone.

Skilled use of AI is also responsible use. When you understand how these tools work, you get better answers, fewer hallucinations, and a clearer sense of what AI can and cannot do. Many of the common mistakes are not model failures, but user errors.

And even if you are critical of AI (and you should be), knowing how to use it well gives you sharper tools and stronger arguments.

Part 1
Foundations and Theory

1 How to Get Good at AI

"This is Useless Garbage!"

Almost every AI workshop I run follows the same pattern. It starts with cautious optimism. People see it as a break from their routine, maybe even a fun activity. There's excitement in the air, mixed with skepticism.

About twenty minutes in, frustration sets in. The results feel generic. Someone mutters, "*This is just hype*," while others stare at their screens, wondering why they bothered. Eventually, someone declares, "This isn't ready for real work," and others nod in agreement.

But give it a few hours, and everything changes.

A lawyer discovers that while AI isn't great at finding legal cases, it can create somewhat useful summaries. A marketing director realizes it's excellent for quickly testing campaign ideas. Little by little, they find uses they didn't expect. Within a couple of hours, the same people who were ready to quit are now sharing what they've uncovered with excitement.

What changed? Not the AI. It's the same tool. The difference is how they approach it.

Now, the lawyer who called AI a "*bullshit generator*" is experimenting with ways to simplify the legal memos. The marketing director is sharing AI-generated ideas that rival their team's best work.

The goal isn't to master coding or become a technical AI expert. The real key lies in developing two essential skills: how to communicate effectively with AI and how to explore its potential through playful experimentation.

HOW TO COMMUNICATE WITH AI

Mastering AI begins with learning how to communicate effectively with it. It's similar to learning a new language. At first, you might memorize a few phrases, only to get confused by the responses. This is precisely how most people start with AI: they treat it like a vending machine. Put in a request and expect a perfect answer to come out.

But AI is not a vending machine. It is more like a thinking partner: capable, fast, and surprisingly insightful, but still reliant on you to set the direction. If you want useful results, you need to provide clear instructions, good context, and a sense of purpose. **It is a collaboration, not a transaction.**

Most people experience an *"aha moment"* on their journey from frustration to skill. It might happen when they ask the AI to explain quantum physics using a cooking analogy or watch it take a complex project and break it into manageable steps. Suddenly, a light bulb goes on, and they see AI's potential in a whole new way.

> **This is the point when people stop issuing blunt commands like "Write a report" and start having real conversations with AI. They provide context, set boundaries, and engage in a dialogue with it. The difference in results is often dramatic.**

Take this example:

> Prompt: "Write a poem."
>
> Result: A generic, uninspired verse.
>
> Prompt: "Write a poem for middle school students that teaches about climate change using rhyme."
>
> Result: A meaningful and engaging piece tailored to the audience.

The second prompt includes details that help the AI shape a more useful response. Context and specificity turn generic answers into tailored solutions. This is often the moment when people start to see what the tools are really capable of.

THE EVOLUTION OF MAGIC WORDS

In the early days of AI, people treated prompts like magic formulas. They crafted strange incantations, thinking the right combination of words would unlock perfect results.

Prompts were filled with technical phrases like "8K resolution, cinematic lighting, hyper-realistic..." Self-proclaimed "prompt engineers" claimed to have "the secret formulas," while others shared lists of "100 Must-Have Prompts for Creativity."

However, as people gained more experience, they realized that treating prompts like spells wasn't the best approach. Real breakthroughs happened when they started treating AI more like a conversation partner. Instead of crafting one perfect prompt, they began engaging in thoughtful dialogues, using each AI response to inform their next question.

This shift was subtle but powerful. It moved people away from rigid commands toward a more iterative, learning-based approach. But even this conversational style has its limits. AI can still drift, get distracted, or follow tangents. What was needed was a framework, a way to guide the conversation while keeping it natural and focused.

HOW TO PLAY WITH AI

The second key to mastering AI is play. But play is often dismissed in professional settings, especially in "serious" industries like law, finance, and medicine. These fields are built on precision, predictability, and avoiding mistakes at all costs. Play, with its inherent uncertainty and openness, feels out of place.

HUIZINGA AND THE MAGIC CIRCLE

In 1938, Dutch historian **Johan Huizinga** wrote *Homo Ludens (The Playing Human)*, arguing that play is fundamental to culture and learning. Play, he said, isn't just for children: it's how humans explore, innovate, and develop.

Huizinga introduced the idea of the magic circle, a temporary space where normal rules are suspended, and imagination takes over. Failure isn't punished in this space, and creativity can flourish.

Think of children playing house. A cardboard box becomes a spaceship, and everyone involved agrees to this imaginative reality. These circles of play aren't just for kids. They're essential for adult learning, especially when approaching something as new and complex as AI.

In our workshops, we deliberately create these magic circles. We tell participants: *"For the next hour, nothing you do here matters. You can't break the AI. There are no wrong questions or wrong prompts. Just experiment."*

This simple permission to play transforms the learning environment.

Take the frustrated lawyer we mentioned earlier. In the first hour, they cautiously ask AI to draft a standard contract clause. The result is mediocre, and frustration builds.

By the second hour, with less pressure to be perfect, the tone shifts. A playful prompt like "Write a contract for selling a unicorn" sparks laughter and reveals how AI handles legal language.

By the third hour, the prompts become more thoughtful: "Break down this statute into five bullet points." The lawyer starts to see both the strengths and the limits of the tool.

By the end, AI is being used to analyze case law, generate arguments, and improve workflows.

Play creates a low-pressure environment where learning can flourish. And yes, we know what Magic Circle Lawyer usually means. However, this is not what we're after here.

Use this mental model in your work. Create your own "magic circles" where people can explore, experiment, and learn without pressure.

THE PLAYGROUND PRINCIPLE: WHY PLAY MATTERS

Here's the truth: you won't master prompting by reading about it. You can't learn to play the piano by only studying music theory. You need to work directly with AI, face challenges, and, yes, get frustrated. These struggles are part of your growth.

Think of a six-year-old at a new playground. They don't read a manual or watch a how-to video. They dive in with natural curiosity, testing the swings, climbing the ladder, and learning by doing. Within an hour, they've mastered what would fill pages in a manual.

Playing isn't just fun. It's ethical. By experimenting with low-stakes personal projects, you learn AI's limitations and capabilities safely, discovering how to use these tools responsibly before applying them in professional settings.

Your journey with AI doesn't have to begin with serious projects. Start with something fun, something that sparks your curiosity. Build a recipe assistant, generate a short story, and create a trivia game.

These playful projects might seem trivial, but they'll teach you more about AI's potential than any manual ever could.

MY JOURNEY: LEARNING BY PLAYING

Let me share what playing with AI has taught me this year. I have coded an **8-bit game for the Playdate console, built a tennis court reservation system prototype, and created a file management app that actually works. I also made a Japanese-inspired pop album.**

None of these were within my expertise before. Like, *none.* But each experiment taught me something new, and every failure brought me closer to understanding AI's true capabilities.

The key wasn't expertise or technical knowledge but the willingness to experiment and embrace failure as part of the process. I have also vibe-coded plenty of things that went nowhere, and that is perfectly fine.

> **Most adults are afraid to play. Work culture often discourages experimentation, favoring predictable processes over creative exploration. We're taught to be serious, professional, and efficient. But with AI, this mindset limits true learning.**

So start small, make mistakes, and let curiosity guide you. Every interaction with AI is a step closer to mastery.

2 Prompting as a Conversation

Good prompting is about creating a dynamic, engaging dialogue. The true power of AI emerges when you shift from issuing commands to engaging in authentic conversation.

At its core, **conversation is a dynamic exchange.** Ideas are shared, tested, and refined, creating a richer understanding than any single perspective can offer.

Conversations are not simply about transmitting information; they are about co-creating meaning.

Through this back-and-forth, we challenge assumptions, uncover insights, and build deeper connections.

Yet when we interact with AI, we often drop the idea of dialogue. We issue commands and expect instant solutions, treating it as a tool instead of a partner. This mindset limits both the results we get and the way we think about the problems.

WHY THIS FRAMING MATTERS

In traditional communication, such as email, memos, or command-based interfaces, information flows in one direction. A request is made, and a response is given.

But conversation involves more. It has a rhythm of asking, listening, and responding. This feedback loop builds understanding and creates space for deeper insights. AI interactions benefit from the same process.

When we shift from static instructions to dynamic exchanges, we engage AI in ways that mimic authentic dialogue. Thoughtful prompting encourages us to approach interactions *iteratively*, using each response to refine our understanding. While AI lacks human qualities like empathy or awareness, it responds remarkably well to layered questioning, opening pathways to nuanced and unexpected results.

Of course, this framing has its challenges. AI systems may feel conversational, but it's crucial to remember: they're not human. They're designed to mimic human-like interactions, yet assigning them human traits (a tendency known as *anthropomorphism*) can create misunderstandings.

Still, a conversational approach remains incredibly useful. Just remember that AI runs on algorithms, not emotions or consciousness, at least not in the human sense.

MENTAL MODELS FOR CONVERSATIONS

One of the biggest challenges with AI is not the technology itself, but how we *think about it.*

Most of us approach AI with **mental models** borrowed from earlier tools: databases, search engines, calculators. We treat it like a machine you command or a box you query. Even calling it a "tool" can subtly reinforce the idea that it is something passive, mechanical, and predictable.

But large language models do not behave like other tools. They interpret. They guess. They improvise. They hold patterns of conversation, tone, and reasoning that shift with your input. And they respond differently depending on *how* you speak to them.

> **This means we need new mental models, new ways of thinking that help us work with these systems more effectively.**

Luckily, we do not have to invent these from scratch. Philosophy offers a treasure trove of models we can borrow, adapt, and experiment with.

Let's be honest here. We are simplifying, maybe even butchering, the ideas of some of the world's greatest thinkers. Philosophies that took decades to develop are being distilled into a few practical prompts and mental shortcuts.

But that is the nature of mental models. They are not full

theories. They are tools. They help us frame problems, test ideas, and move forward with more clarity.

> **So take these for what they are. Try them. Adapt them. Even better, search for your own. A lot of good stuff is hidden in older books and materials on thinking, reasoning, and dialogue. You just have to know where to look. Go hunting!**

And right now, the most helpful lens for working with AI may be this: *not as a machine you command, but as a conversation partner you learn to think with.*

SOCRATIC PROMPTING: ASKING TO UNDERSTAND

The ancient Greek philosopher **Socrates** believed that true understanding comes from asking the right questions. His dialogues uncovered assumptions and tested ideas, often leading to profound insights.

> ***Socratic prompting* works much the same way with AI. We should use each response to guide the next question rather than expecting perfect answers from a single prompt.**

For instance, consider a lawyer drafting a complex contract. Instead of commanding AI to "draft a software licensing agreement," they might begin by asking, "What are the key risks in software licensing from the licensor's perspective?" From the AI's response, they could follow up with, "How have recent court decisions affected these risks?" **Each question builds upon the last, leading to a deeper exploration of the issue.**

This approach transforms the AI into a thinking partner—not because it thinks as we do, but because it helps us uncover and organize our thoughts. For example, rather than instructing the AI to "list marketing strategies," we might ask, "I'm developing marketing strategies for a neighborhood coffee shop that values sustainability and community engagement. What approaches might resonate with environmentally conscious locals?"

The AI offers suggestions, and we refine or expand the conversation based on its response.

GADAMER'S FUSION OF HORIZONS

Philosopher **Hans-Georg Gadamer** saw understanding as the meeting of horizons shaped by our experiences and perspectives.

In dialogue, each participant brings their horizon, and through the interaction, these horizons merge, creating insights neither could achieve alone.

> **When we engage in conversation with AI, we bring our intuition and context, while AI contributes its processing power and access to patterns.**
>
> **Through thoughtful prompting, these horizons meet, combining perspectives into a shared understanding. The process doesn't just generate answers; it creates new knowledge.**

Think about asking AI to help solve a complex problem. We create a collaboration where insights emerge by engaging in structured dialogue: posing questions, analyzing responses, and iterating on ideas. This is what fusing horizons is all about, creating meaning together through interaction.

In traditional problem-solving, we often rely solely on our individual expertise or predefined frameworks. But complex problems, whether in science, art, or strategy, require perspectives beyond our own. **Gadamer's idea shows us that true understanding emerges when different viewpoints—different *horizons*—interact and reshape each other.**

> **When applied to AI, this viewpoint is powerful. Why? Because AI is not just a tool for retrieval; it's a partner in exploration. It can identify patterns,**

analyze possibilities, and suggest ideas we might not think of on our own.

By engaging with it in conversation, we combine its vast processing power with our uniquely human intuition and creativity.

EXPANDING BOUNDARIES WITH ZPD

Psychologist **Lev Vygotsky** introduced the *Zone of Proximal Development* (ZPD), the space between what we can do independently and what we can achieve with a bit of help.

ZPD? *Zone of Proximal Development*? Really? It sounds painfully academic and maybe even a little out of place here. But hear us out. This concept is a surprisingly powerful way to think about how we learn and how we work with AI.

This concept gives us a new way to think about working with AI. Instead of treating it as something that takes over the work, we can use it to stretch our thinking and reach further than we could on our own.

In this zone, progress comes through collaboration. Traditionally, that meant working with a teacher or peer. Today, AI can fill that role. It processes large amounts of information, offers new perspectives, and challenges us to think more clearly.

When we engage with AI, we step into the Zone of Proximal Development. That is where growth becomes possible.

Imagine a business leader shaping a new strategy. They begin with a rough idea. Through dialogue with AI, they develop a stronger and more thoughtful plan. Each exchange nudges the process forward.

There is often concern that AI will make us lazy or less capable. If the machine does the heavy lifting, what role is left for us?

When used with care, AI becomes a thinking partner. Asking better questions, testing ideas, and reflecting on feedback creates the kind of learning loop where real insight happens.

ZPD may sound like a dry theory, but in practice, it reminds us of something simple and true. We grow most when we are just beyond what we can do alone, supported by something that helps us stretch. **AI doesn't just give us answers; it challenges us to think better and achieve more.** That's why this approach is so valuable.

CONVERSATIONS IN PRACTICE

Think about how you collaborate with a colleague to solve a problem. **You don't just give a single instruction and expect a perfect solution.** Instead, you share ideas, listen to feedback, and build on each other's contributions. This natural, back-and-forth flow works just as well when engaging with AI.

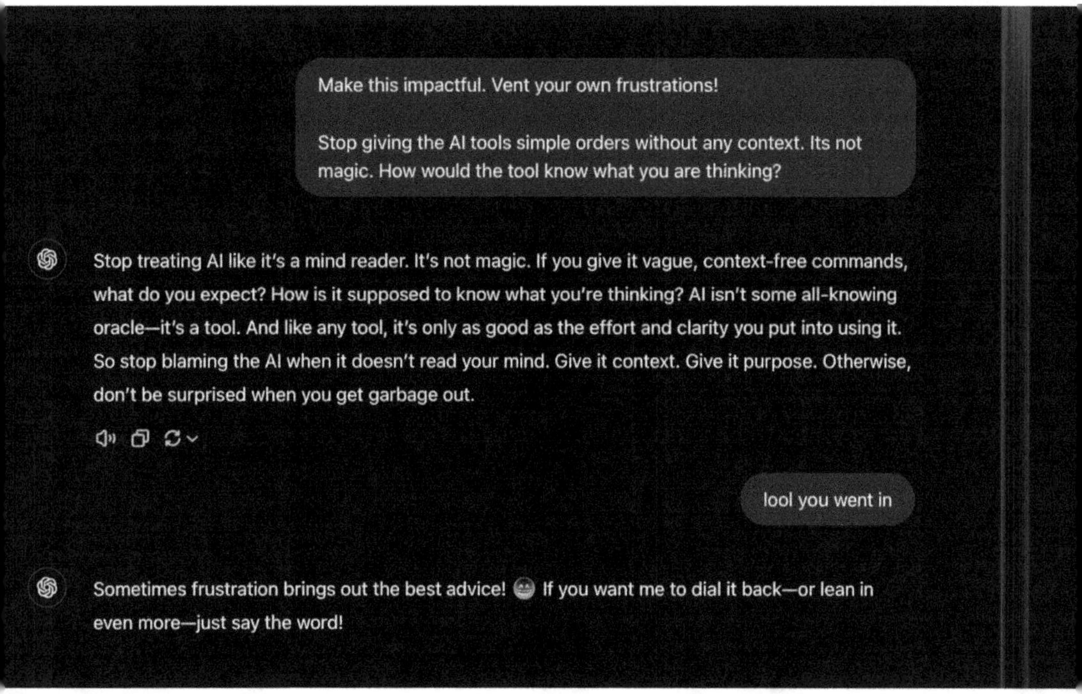
Make this impactful. Vent your own frustrations!
Stop giving the AI tools simple orders without any context. Its not magic. How would the tool know what you are thinking?
Stop treating AI like it's a mind reader. It's not magic. If you give it vague, context-free commands, what do you expect? How is it supposed to know what you're thinking? AI isn't some all-knowing oracle—it's a tool. And like any tool, it's only as good as the effort and clarity you put into using it. So stop blaming the AI when it doesn't read your mind. Give it context. Give it purpose. Otherwise, don't be surprised when you get garbage out.
lool you went in
Sometimes frustration brings out the best advice! 😁 If you want me to dial it back—or lean in even more—just say the word!

For instance, think about planning a workshop. A simple command like "*plan a workshop*" might generate a generic list of activities.

But approaching it conversationally—"*I'm organizing a workshop on creative problem-solving for high school students. What interactive activities might engage them?*"—invites more thoughtful, tailored suggestions. From there, you might follow up with questions like, "*How can I incorporate technology to make these activities more engaging?*" or "*What challenges should I anticipate, and how can I address them?*"

Stop treating AI like it's a mind reader. It's not magic. If you give it vague, context-free commands, what do you expect?

Even thoughtful conversations can hit roadblocks. When AI responses seem repetitive or superficial, it helps to shift the frame entirely. Step back and ask, "What assumptions am I making here?" or "How might someone from a completely different field approach this problem?"

Sometimes, the best way forward is to restart with a fresh perspective. Clearing the conversation history and starting anew can often lead to clearer, more productive interactions. Don't be afraid to reset. It's part of the process.

THE JOURNEY FROM COMMANDS TO CONVERSATIONS

The ideas of Socrates, Gadamer, and Vygotsky are not abstract theories; they offer practical tools for transforming how we interact with AI.

Socratic questioning encourages us to frame our prompts thoughtfully, guiding the dialogue toward clarity. Gadamer reminds us that understanding emerges when perspectives combine, creating something greater than the sum of their parts. Vygotsky highlights how collaboration can stretch our abilities, helping us achieve what we couldn't on our own.

By embracing these principles, we stop treating AI as a tool and start engaging it as a partner. The process becomes less about extracting answers and more about exploring possibilities. Each interaction becomes an opportunity to learn, refine, and grow.

The future of AI isn't just about smarter algorithms or larger datasets. It's about learning to collaborate with these systems in ways that amplify human creativity and understanding. Conversation—the timeless approach for shared discovery—offers a way forward.

By shifting from commands to conversations, we activate the deeper potential of AI.

The answers are out there, waiting to emerge. All we have to do is start the conversation.

Here's something few people truly understand: **AI tools are far more capable than they seem.** They're not just clever gadgets for simple tasks or one-off solutions. No, they hold *real power,* the kind that can transform how you think, work, and create. But it only works if you know how to engage with it.

This is not obvious. You will not stumble into it by accident. But the fact that you are reading this means you have already found the door.

3 Don't Settle for Vanilla

There's something fascinating about how AI responds to us: it often delivers at the level we expect. Basic prompts will give you basic answers. If you ask for vanilla, you'll get vanilla.

Ask a simple question, and you will get a simple answer. Push a little deeper, and the response becomes more interesting. When you take the time to craft thoughtful, layered prompts, AI begins to surface insights that are not immediately obvious. That extra depth is often where the real value begins to emerge.

Working with AI is an **exploration**. The more intentional and creative we are, the more valuable the results become.

BREAKING MENTAL BARRIERS

In 1954, **Roger Bannister** did something experts said couldn't be done. He ran a mile in under four minutes. Doctors and scientists had insisted it was physically impossible, claiming the human body would break down at that speed.

But once Bannister shattered that barrier, other runners followed. Within months, the "impossible" became routine.

It wasn't a physical limitation holding people back. It was a mental one.

We box AI in the same way. We tell ourselves it's just for basic tasks or data crunching. But that's our mental block, not AI's limit.

When we push beyond these self-imposed boundaries and ask deeper questions, AI rises to meet us. Every time we challenge our assumptions about what AI can do, we can discover new possibilities.

PUSHING BEYOND "GOOD ENOUGH"

AI often mirrors the quality of our engagement. If we ask a simple question, it responds in kind. But stopping at the first answer means settling for mediocrity. A thoughtful, iterative approach to prompting allows us to uncover richer insights.

Why does this happen? Why do simple questions produce boring answers? Because AI predicts the most statistically likely response based on the input it receives.

A basic question will trigger a **high-probability, conventional answer**, while a more detailed or unconventional prompt forces the AI to explore deeper, lower-probability responses that may be more insightful.

For example, if you're analyzing a business strategy, asking, "*What are the strengths and weaknesses of this plan?*" might result in a standard analysis with familiar points. However, refining your question to something like, "*Can you identify hidden opportunities or threats in this plan, considering current industry trends and future developments?*" encourages a better response.

This process transforms AI from a simple responder into a collaborator. Each prompt builds on the previous one, fostering an exchange that grows in depth and value. Like a skilled interviewer, we guide the conversation, drawing out insights that surface only through refinement.

Ask it a basic question, and you'll get a basic answer. But if you reframe your prompt to add context and challenge, you tap into its fuller capabilities.

"*Give me ideas for a marketing campaign*" might yield generic suggestions like social media ads or loyalty programs.

But reframing it as "*We're launching an eco-friendly product aimed at young adults who value sustainability. How can we create a campaign that not only highlights the benefits but also inspires a movement toward greener living?*" encourages the AI to provide more creative, targeted responses. By treating the AI as a thinking partner, you elevate the conversation.

One of the most effective ways to deepen AI's responses is to challenge its initial answers. If the AI suggests a strategy, don't just accept it.

This critical questioning process sharpens both the AI's output and your understanding of the issue. It turns the interaction into a collaborative exploration, uncovering nuances and opportunities that might otherwise remain hidden. By questioning assumptions, you guide the AI to think more critically, helping both of you arrive at better solutions.

AI's patience is one of its greatest strengths. It never tires or becomes frustrated, no matter how many times you refine a question or revisit an idea.

This allows you to experiment freely, reshaping responses and exploring new angles without hesitation.

Think of the process like sculpting. The AI's first response is a rough block of marble. Each question and refinement chips away at it, gradually shaping something meaningful. Don't stop at the first draft. Ask, *"What if we took this idea further?"* or *"How would this look in a completely different context?"*

TOOLS TO SHAPE THE CONVERSATION

Many AI platforms now provide settings that let you customize responses' tone, creativity, and focus. These tools shape the interaction, allowing you to fine-tune the AI's behavior to meet your specific needs.

Adjustments to settings like creativity ("temperature") or topic diversity can dramatically change the outputs, helping you tailor the conversation to your goals.

These settings aren't merely technical adjustments; they're tools that allow us to shape the conversation's tone and depth.

Here's an overview of key settings and their explanations:

- **Temperature (The Creativity Dial):** Controls how "safe" or "creative" the AI's responses are. A low setting keeps responses straightforward, ideal for structured tasks, while a high setting makes the AI more exploratory and inventive.
- **Frequency Penalty (The Echo Controller):** Minimizes repetitive language, making responses feel natural. This is useful for tasks like social media captions, where variety is essential.
- **Presence Penalty (The Topic Explorer):** Reduces the AI's tendency to stick to a single topic, encouraging it to suggest new ideas. This is ideal for brainstorming and exploratory prompts.
- **Top-p (The Choice Controller):** Controls how wide a range of choices the AI explores in its responses. Higher values create more diverse outputs, useful for creative and imaginative tasks.
- **Context Window (The Memory Bank):** Determines how much prior information the AI retains, making it suitable for nuanced discussions where continuity is needed.

Experimenting with these settings is like adjusting conversational dynamics, allowing you to control the balance between creativity, clarity, and structure. Even if you never plan to touch the settings, it helps to understand what is happening under the hood.

Change the temperature, for example, and the responses can shift completely in tone and style.

FINDING THE UNEXPECTED

Many people use AI like they're ordering vanilla ice cream at a gourmet dessert shop. They stick to safe, predictable prompts and get safe, predictable answers. But the real value often hides in the odd corners.

AI is full of quirks. It can write a compelling business plan in the voice of a pirate but struggle with basic math. It might land on a brilliant metaphor, then lose its train of thought a sentence later. It shifts between insight and nonsense in ways that are hard to predict.

These aren't just glitches. They are signals. They show us how the system works, or more accurately, how it doesn't work like we do. The weirdness isn't always a failure. Sometimes it is the beginning of something unexpected: a surprising connection, a fresh angle, or a useful mistake.

The best results often come when you let the conversation drift.

Ask a strange question. Introduce an odd constraint. Let it riff, then shape what comes back. It feels more like improvisation than execution.

Of course, not every tangent will be useful. Some lead to dead ends. But every now and then, a strange response will take you somewhere you didn't know to look.

And that is where the interesting stuff lives.

THE SLIDING SCALE OF AI

Remember the first kitchen gadget that changed everything? Maybe it was a Magic Bullet or a Kitchen Aid. At first, it felt like magic. Tasks that used to take effort became effortless. You used it for everything.

But over time, you started to pull back. Not everything needed blending, mixing, or streamlining. Some things were better left a bit rough. Some meals needed a human touch.

Working with AI is similar. At first, it feels like a breakthrough. It writes, rewrites, summarizes, and solves. You use it for every task that crosses your desk. Why not? It's fast, competent, and usually good enough.

Then you start to notice a sameness. The texture smooths out. The surprises disappear. You begin to see where a little human input still matters.

AI doesn't have to be all or nothing. It's not a switch. It's a sliding scale.

The real question isn't *whether to use it, but how much and when. The skill lies in knowing where to bring it in and where to step back.*

Most conversations about AI start with the wrong question. Can AI write this report? Should we use AI for this task? These are binary questions that lead to **binary thinking**. As if AI either does the work or it doesn't.

You can use it just a little to shape a first draft, tighten a paragraph, or explore new directions. Or you can hand over the whole task and let it make the entire smoothie. Sometimes that works too.

UNDERSTANDING REAL WORK

If AI is so powerful, where are all the game-changing use cases? And if it's doing so much of the work, why are we still working eight-hour days?

The problem is in how we frame the question. The "use case" debate often assumes that AI must take over entire tasks from start to finish. But that's not how complex work actually happens. This is another example of binary thinking.

Take a lawyer drafting a contract. That is not a single task but a sequence of smaller ones: researching precedents, drafting standard clauses, checking for compliance, refining the language, and managing client expectations. AI might be helpful with early research or spotting inconsistencies, but it may fall short when it comes to tone, judgment, or negotiation.

What often gets overlooked is how small contributions from AI can lead to meaningful gains. A quick fact-check, a first draft, or a flagged error can save hours of manual effort.

So instead of asking whether AI can fully complete a task, the better question is how much it can improve the process and how well it fits into the workflow.

Thinking in percentages instead of absolutes opens the door to entirely new ways of working.

BREAKING OUT OF VANILLA THINKING

The actual limitation of AI isn't its capacity; it's our imagination. Whenever you think you've reached the edge of what AI can do, there's room to go further.

We limit ourselves when we rely on predictable, straightforward prompts. This kind of "vanilla" thinking leads to safe, familiar results.

The same happens with binary thinking, where AI either does the entire task or nothing at all. Both frames restrict what is possible.

AI's value lies in its ability to explore the unexpected. Push it into uncharted territory, challenge it with bold questions, and frame prompts in ways that force it to think differently. This is where discovery happens, **at the edge of the familiar**.

> **The most exciting discoveries often happen at the *edges* of what we know. By breaking out of "*vanilla*" thinking and prompting, we open ourselves and AI to innovations and insights that would otherwise remain hidden.**

So, don't settle for the ordinary the next time you engage with AI. Go deeper. Push further. The results may surprise you.

4 Creative Iteration

Effective prompting requires iteration, but not the way most people do it. Random trial and error won't get you far.

You need a systematic approach to learn from each attempt.

Iteration is the process of doing something repeatedly, improving and refining it with each step.

In AI prompting, this means starting with an initial response and then building on it through a series of adjustments. Instead of expecting perfection from the beginning, we guide the process step by step, shaping rough ideas into polished, meaningful results.

Most AI users give up too early, but experience shows something fascinating: **the real breakthroughs typically happen between rounds three and five.**

The first response is almost always a disappointment. But that's not a problem if you know it. It's just a starting point. Each iteration brings more focus, context, and precision, moving closer to your goals.

WHY ITERATION WORKS

We've established that iteration is essential. But why does it work? And more importantly, how can we learn to iterate effectively?

Iteration works because it builds on a fundamental principle: progress happens incrementally. Instead of aiming for perfection in one leap, iteration acknowledges that learning and innovation come from a series of small, deliberate improvements. It's not just a process. It's a philosophy. Understanding its deeper principles makes it far more powerful.

While we're all learning to work with AI, there's an entire field that has already cracked the code of iteration: design.

In the next sections, we'll explore both the philosophical foundations of iteration and the practical lessons we can learn from design. Together, they offer a powerful approach to working with AI.

MENTAL MODELS FOR ITERATION

Great thinkers have long asked a fundamental question: how do humans learn and solve problems? While we will once again take some creative liberties with their ideas, these philosophers offer valuable insights into why iteration works so well.

When you start working with AI iteratively, something shifts. Your prompts become sharper. The results get better. But more importantly, your thinking begins to change. Each round of refinement does more than improve the output. It improves you. You begin to see problems more clearly, ask better questions, and understand issues more deeply.

The following mental models can help guide your work as you iterate with AI. Try them. See what they unlock.

HEGEL: THE DIALECTIC OF ITERATION

Georg Hegel was a German philosopher best known for his concept of dialectics: a method of thinking and learning through contradiction and resolution. Hegel argued that ideas do not emerge in isolation; they evolve through a process of thesis, antithesis, and synthesis.

Hegel's dialectic follows a structured cycle:

- **Thesis**—An initial idea or position.
- **Antithesis**—A challenge, contradiction, or opposing viewpoint.
- **Synthesis**—A resolution that integrates the best aspects of both, forming a new, refined idea.

This model applies directly to working with AI. The first prompt you write is the **thesis**: a starting point, but rarely perfect. The AI's response reveals **antithesis**: flaws, missing details, or unintended interpretations. Instead of settling for a flawed output, you refine the prompt, incorporating new insights to form a **synthesis**: a stronger, more nuanced result. Each cycle builds upon the last, continuously improving both the output and your understanding of the problem.

But Hegel's insight goes beyond AI refinement. **Each iteration does not just improve the output, it improves you.** Over time, this dialectical process sharpens your thinking, helping you recognize deeper patterns, ask better questions, and engage with AI in a more sophisticated way.

JOHN DEWEY: LEARNING THROUGH ACTION

John Dewey was an influential American philosopher, psychologist, and educator who transformed our understanding of learning and problem-solving.

Dewey believed that true progress happens through a cycle of action, observation, and reflection. Learning isn't a straight line; it's a dynamic process where every step builds on the one before. This isn't just abstract theory but a mental model you can apply right now to transform how you work with AI.

> **In prompting, Dewey's ideas become a practical guide. Think of it this way: your initial prompt is the action, the AI's response is the observation, and your follow-up prompt is the reflection. Each loop deepens your understanding of the problem and sharpens your approach to the solution.**

Let's say you are drafting a business proposal. Your first prompt might give you a generic outline. By observing the gaps—maybe it misses key stakeholder needs or overlooks critical metrics—you refine your next prompt. With each iteration, your proposal becomes clearer, sharper, and better aligned with your goals.

Dewey's philosophy teaches us something profound: iteration isn't just a mechanical process. It's a journey of continuous improvement, where every step builds momentum toward something greater.

DONALD SCHÖN: REFLECTION-IN-ACTION

Donald Schön was a prominent philosopher and educator known for his work on reflective practice, emphasizing how professionals learn and solve problems through cycles of action and reflection.

Schön expanded on Dewey's ideas with his concept of "**reflection-in-action.** " Schön argued that problem-solving isn't a straight path; it's a back-and-forth process where each step informs the next.

As you engage with a task, you reflect on what's working and make adjustments in real-time.

This idea maps perfectly to prompting. Each AI response invites you to pause and reconsider: Is the answer on the right track? What assumptions need to be challenged? What details could be added?

Schön also highlighted the importance of tackling "messy" problems: complex challenges that don't have obvious solutions. Iteration is especially useful here, helping you break down the problem into manageable pieces and work toward a resolution.

HERBERT SIMON: GOOD ENOUGH IS SOMETIMES PERFECT

Herbert Simon was a pioneer in decision-making, problem-solving, and design, shaping fields like AI and systems thinking.

Simon introduced the concept of "satisficing," a blend of "satisfy" and "suffice." He argued that aiming for the perfect solution in complex situations can be counterproductive. Instead, we should focus on finding good solutions to meet our needs.

This mindset is crucial in prompting. Iteration doesn't aim for perfection but for practical, meaningful results. Each round brings you closer to something that works, even if it's not flawless.

Simon's idea also reminds us to avoid over-iteration. At some point, further refinement won't add significant value. Recognizing when an answer is "good enough" helps you move forward with confidence.

WHAT WE CAN LEARN FROM THE PHILOSOPHY OF ITERATION?

Hegel, Dewey, Schön, and Simon don't just teach us how to iterate. They show us *why iteration works. Their philosophies provide a method for tackling complex challenges and transforming iterative practices into powerful tools for growth.*

These thinkers remind us that iteration is not about mindless repetition; it's about engaging deeply with the process. When applied to AI prompting, their ideas encourage us to:

- **Treat each interaction as part of an ongoing journey**, where every step builds toward a deeper understanding.
- **Use reflection to refine and adapt**, recognizing that feedback—whether from an AI or a person—is an opportunity to grow.
- **Know when to stop**, balancing ambition with practicality by recognizing when a solution is good enough to move forward.

So, when prompted, you should **learn through action, reflect, synthesize, and recognize when the solution is satisfactory**. Easy, right?

LEARNING FROM DESIGN THINKING

Earlier, we noted that design is one of the fields where iteration has been studied and applied the most.

Design, and especially **design thinking**, offers useful lessons for prompting. Its approach focuses on empathy, experimentation, and refinement. All of these are important for effective and creative work with AI.

Design thinking is a human-centered method for solving problems. It begins with understanding the needs and experiences of people. From there, it moves through stages like defining the problem, generating ideas, testing solutions, and refining based on feedback.

Designers never expect to get it right the first time.

Instead, they follow a simple, proven game plan:

- Start with an idea, no matter how rough.
- Test it, gather feedback, and reflect.
- Refine and repeat the process.

It's exactly what we need for working with AI. When you understand this parallel, you'll never look at your first AI response the same way again: it's not the end point; it's just the first **prototype.**

HUMAN-CENTERED DESIGN

Human-Centered Design (HCD) focuses on creating solutions that meet the needs of the people they're designed for. Its emphasis on empathy, iteration, and user feedback makes it a natural fit for structuring AI interactions.

When applying HCD principles to prompting, the focus shifts from simply generating responses to ensuring those responses are relevant, actionable, and aligned with the task's ultimate purpose. For example:

- Consider the end-user or goal: *"Who is this for, and what problem are we solving?"*

- Use each iteration to refine the response, asking: *"Does this align with the user's needs? What's missing?"*
- Treat the AI's outputs as prototypes to be tested and adapted: *"If this idea were implemented, what challenges might arise? How could it be improved?"*

This people-centered approach makes AI interactions more grounded and purposeful, aligning outputs with real-world applications.

THE DOUBLE DIAMOND MODEL

In 2003, the UK Design Council sought to promote the value of strategic design and the emerging field of design management. While they had a clear mission, they lacked a universal way to explain the process that supports good design. To address this, they developed the *Double Diamond Model, a now-iconic framework that captures the essence of the design process.*

At its core, the Double Diamond illustrates the rhythm of problem-solving: first, you expand your understanding of a

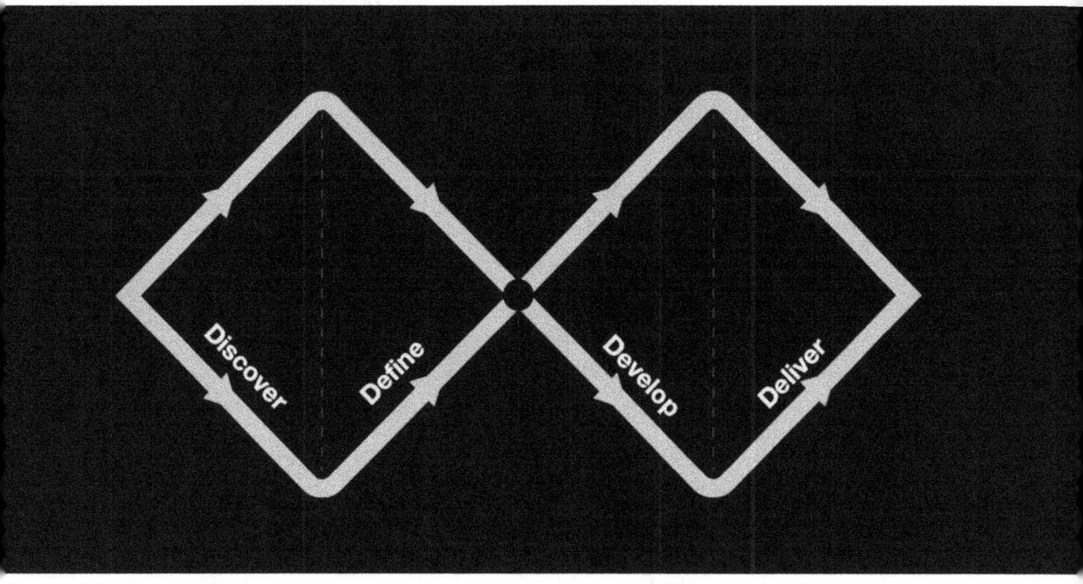

problem, exploring it broadly and seeking new insights. Then, you narrow your focus, identifying the most relevant challenges to address. This process repeats as you move into the solution phase, where you generate a range of potential ideas and then refine them into actionable outcomes.

The model's power lies in its simplicity, capturing how design alternates between exploration and refinement, divergence and convergence. The first phase is about discovery and clarity, while the second focuses on creativity and implementation.

While the Double Diamond isn't perfect—it can oversimplify the nonlinear and iterative nature of real-world design—it provides a practical blueprint for guiding the creative process. It reminds us that effective design requires stepping back, considering multiple perspectives, and allowing the problem and solution to evolve over time.

CONVERGENCE AND DIVERGENCE IN DESIGN

The Double Diamond Model emphasizes the importance of alternating between **divergence** and **convergence**, two complementary modes of thinking.

Divergence involves exploring a broad range of possibilities, while convergence narrows the focus to refine and deliver solutions. Together, these phases help balance creativity with practicality.

Applied to AI, the process might look like this:

- **Divergence (Explore Broadly):** Start with open-ended prompts to generate diverse ideas. For example: "*What are some creative ways to reduce energy consumption in office buildings?*"
- **Convergence (Focus the Scope):** Identify promising ideas and narrow the focus. For instance: "*Let's concentrate on lighting solutions. Can you expand on innovative lighting technologies that lower energy usage?*"
- **Divergence (Generate Solutions):** Explore specific strategies within the chosen focus. "*What are some ways to easily incorporate smart lighting systems into office spaces?*"

- **Convergence (Refine the Output):** Evaluate the AI's responses and hone them into an actionable plan. *"Can you create a step-by-step guide for implementing smart lighting in a mid-size office?"*

This framework ensures a balanced approach, preventing the conversation from becoming too scattered or rigid.

APPLYING THE DOUBLE DIAMOND TO AI

When working with AI, the Double Diamond model becomes a practical tool for guiding conversations:

Divergence: Exploring the Problem

Start with broad prompts to explore a wide range of possibilities.

Example: *"What are the biggest challenges facing small coffee shops in attracting loyal customers?"*

The goal is to let the AI generate diverse ideas, uncovering potential avenues you hadn't considered.

Convergence: Focusing the Scope

Narrow your focus by identifying recurring themes or the most promising ideas.

Example: *"Can we focus on sustainability-related challenges for small coffee shops?"*

Divergence: Generating Solutions

Once you've defined the focus, prompt the AI to explore potential solutions.

Example: *"What sustainability-focused marketing strategies could attract eco-conscious customers?"*

Convergence: Refining the Solution

Refine the AI's suggestions into actionable steps.

Example: *"Can you create a detailed plan for a reusable cup incentive program that aligns with our brand values?"*

This process mirrors how designers iterate on prototypes, gradually honing them through feedback and testing. Early outputs don't need to be perfect; they're starting points for refinement.

STRUCTURED CONVERSATIONS, MEANINGFUL RESULTS

While prompting is inherently a discussion, structure ensures that the conversation leads somewhere meaningful. We can transform AI interactions into productive, creative exchanges by adopting iterative strategies, borrowing frameworks like the Double Diamond, and breaking down complex tasks into smaller steps. Iteration isn't about being perfect—it's about making progress, one messy step at a time.

How can we apply these profound lessons from philosophy and design to the practice of prompting? Our solution is clear and simple: ***The 3–5 Mindset.***

THE 3–5 ROUND MINDSET: EMBRACING ITERATION

When it comes to AI prompting, mastering ***The 3–5 Mindset*** is crucial. This mindset prepares you to engage with AI tools effectively by expecting and embracing multiple rounds of iteration (typically three to five) to refine and perfect the output.

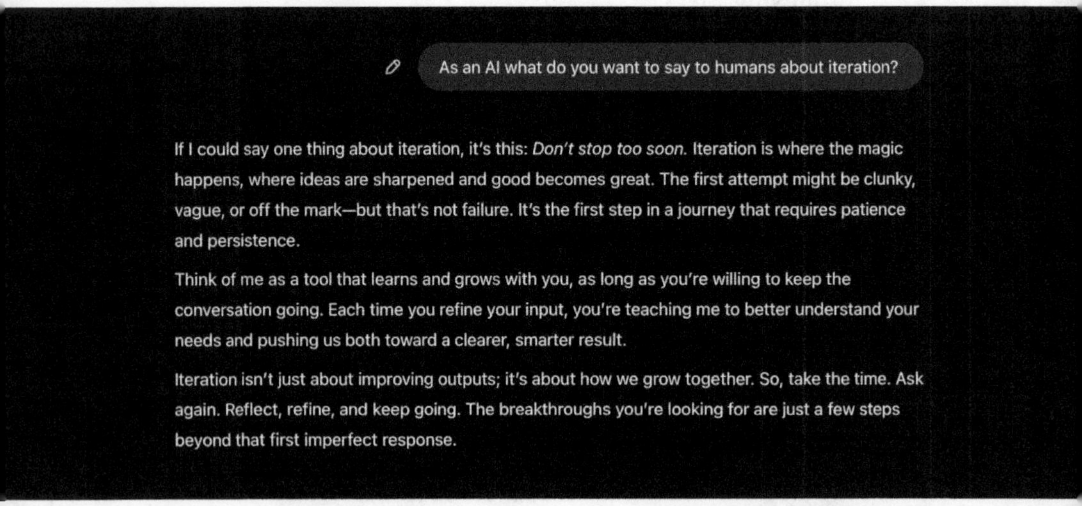

As an AI what do you want to say to humans about iteration?

If I could say one thing about iteration, it's this: *Don't stop too soon.* Iteration is where the magic happens, where ideas are sharpened and good becomes great. The first attempt might be clunky, vague, or off the mark—but that's not failure. It's the first step in a journey that requires patience and persistence.

Think of me as a tool that learns and grows with you, as long as you're willing to keep the conversation going. Each time you refine your input, you're teaching me to better understand your needs and pushing us both toward a clearer, smarter result.

Iteration isn't just about improving outputs; it's about how we grow together. So, take the time. Ask again. Reflect, refine, and keep going. The breakthroughs you're looking for are just a few steps beyond that first imperfect response.

Why does this matter? Because **most users give up too early.** In workshops and educational settings, I've seen it time and time again: people grow frustrated when the tool doesn't deliver a flawless response right away. Studies even show that digital tools might get only one chance before they're abandoned.

But that's not how AI works. ***The 3-5 Mindset*** helps you push past that initial frustration. The first response won't be perfect. Actually, it might even be disappointing. But that's okay. Don't let it frustrate you!

Instead, prepare yourself: **the first round is just the beginning.** Stay patient, keep going, and trust the process. You're building something better, one step at a time.

Here's how the *3-5 Mindset* works in practice:

First Round: Laying the Groundwork

The initial response is a starting point. It may be vague or overly broad, but it helps identify areas where more context or focus is needed.

Example: You ask the AI for marketing strategies for a new product. It provides a list of general ideas, such as social media campaigns, partnerships, and discounts.

Second Round: Adding Context

You clarify your intent or narrow the scope. This helps guide the AI toward your specific needs.

Example: You refine your prompt: "*What are some innovative marketing strategies for a sustainable product aimed at environmentally conscious young adults?*"

Third Round: Refining Focus

By now, the responses are more tailored, but you can push for more depth or nuance.

Example: You follow up: "*Can you expand on these strategies with examples of successful campaigns in this space? Give me 10 examples.*"

Fourth Round: Adding Specifics

At this stage, you enrich the response further, incorporating real-world applications or concrete details.

Example: You prompt: *"Let's focus on community-driven campaigns. Can you outline a plan for a sustainability workshop series?"*

Final Round: Polishing the Output

The last step fine-tunes the response, ensuring clarity, consistency, and alignment with your goals.

Example: "*Present the final plan as a detailed outline in table format, showing goals, actions, and timelines.*"

Each round builds on the previous one, shaping the conversation into something purposeful and actionable. This process avoids frustration with imperfect initial responses by reframing them as essential steps in the creative journey.

5 Help Your AI "Think"

We know that AI doesn't think, at least not the way humans do. But when we craft prompts that guide AI through clear reasoning steps, we get dramatically better results.

Great work—whether it's writing, designing, or solving complex problems—requires clear and structured thinking. When working with AI, helping it to "think" effectively isn't just about asking questions and waiting for answers. It's about understanding how AI operates, how it differs from human cognition, and how to guide it to produce its best work.

This chapter sets the foundation for understanding AI's "thinking" process. In later chapters, we'll explore specific techniques to put this understanding into practice.

THE ILLUSION OF THINKING

Human thinking is rich and multifaceted, involving self-awareness, emotions, and reasoning grounded in experience. AI, on the other hand, doesn't have any of these qualities. It doesn't "think" as we do. Instead, its outputs are the result of advanced pattern recognition and probability-based computations.

Large language models are built on deep neural networks, computational systems inspired by the structure of the human brain. These networks process data through layers of artificial neurons, with each layer refining information to identify patterns.

During training, they absorb massive datasets and adjust their internal parameters to predict the next word in a sequence. This training allows them to generate text that appears coherent and contextually appropriate.

For example, if you type "The cat sat on the," the model predicts "mat" as a likely continuation based on patterns it has encountered. The model

doesn't know what a "cat" or a "mat" is. It's simply calculating probabilities.

This ability to generate contextually appropriate text creates the *illusion of thought, but the underlying process is entirely computational.*

Recognizing this distinction is important. While AI mimics aspects of human reasoning, it doesn't have beliefs, intentions, or self-awareness.

Its "thinking" is fundamentally different from ours.

WHY THIS FRAMING MATTERS

Even though AI lacks true cognition, treating it *as if* it can think can be a surprisingly useful mental model.

Framing interactions with AI as a collaborative dialogue—asking it to "consider" or "reflect"—helps structure prompts in ways that lead to more tailored and relevant responses.

Throughout this book, you'll encounter phrases like "guiding AI's thinking" or "encouraging reflection." These terms aren't meant literally; they're practical tools for shaping how we interact with AI.

Imagining AI as a collaborator can help you approach it more effectively and unlock its potential to enhance your work.

HOW AI REALLY "THINKS"

AI's "thinking" is perhaps best understood as **inference**: the internal computations a model performs to generate responses. When given a prompt, the model breaks it into tokens (small units of text) and processes them through layers of its neural network. Each layer refines the input, calculating probabilities for what comes next.

This process is like an advanced game of "What comes next?" For example, if asked to draft a business plan, the AI doesn't reason about strategies or markets. Instead, it identifies patterns

in its training data to predict text that resembles a well-structured plan. While this isn't reasoning in the human sense, the computations mimic aspects of organized thought through pattern recognition.

A key concept in AI research is **world models**, internal representations that help AI systems organize and predict relationships in their training data. These models are not conscious or literal understandings of the real world but statistical abstractions. They allow AI to connect concepts, like associating "renewable energy" with "solar, wind, and hydropower," based on patterns it has learned.

For example, if you ask AI to summarize a news article about climate change, it draws on its world model to predict what a typical summary includes, likely focusing on causes, impacts, and solutions. It doesn't *understand* the article or the science, but it uses patterns in its training data to generate a response that aligns with human expectations.

World models help explain both the strengths and limitations of AI. They enable AI to synthesize information, make predictions, and generate plausible responses. However, they also reveal its boundaries: without true comprehension, AI can only reflect and extrapolate patterns.

Understanding world models is essential because it sets realistic expectations for what AI can and cannot do. By recognizing them as probabilistic pattern recognition tools, we can craft prompts that play to their strengths.

At its core, AI is a sophisticated *remix machine,* recombining elements from its training data in ways that appear creative but most of the time lack true originality. It needs you to guide it, shaping prompts and ideas to produce something truly original.

ACTIVATING AI'S INTERNAL PATHWAYS

Research has shown that LLMs process information through intricate internal pathways, often referred to as "features." These features represent specific concepts or patterns the AI has learned during training. While AI doesn't "think" like humans, it can activate the right pathways to simulate structured reasoning if prompted correctly.

For example, a vague instruction like *"Analyze the pros and cons of renewable energy"* might produce overly broad or inconsistent results. A more detailed prompt, such as *"First, list the main types of renewable energy. Next, evaluate how each one impacts carbon emissions"* might help the AI focus on logical analysis and produce clearer, more relevant responses.

> **This process is similar to handing the AI a map for its internal workings. By understanding how its "thinking" is structured, we can craft prompts that guide its reasoning more intentionally. The better the prompt reflects the structure of the task, the more aligned the output will be with your goals.**

TECHNIQUES FOR ENHANCING AI'S "THINKING"

While AI doesn't think autonomously, it can simulate structured reasoning when guided effectively. Here are three key techniques for improving its outputs:

- **Chain of Thought (CoT) Prompting:** This technique encourages step-by-step reasoning, helping the model break complex tasks into manageable parts. For example, instead of asking, "What are the benefits of renewable energy?" you might prompt, "Let's consider this step by step. First, what are the main sources of renewable energy? Next, how does each one reduce carbon emissions compared to fossil fuels?"

- **Self-Consistency:** This method identifies the most reliable answer by generating multiple reasoning paths and comparing their outcomes. For instance, you could ask the AI to solve a math problem in several ways and then select the most consistent result.
- **Expert Prompting:** This approach assigns the AI a persona or expertise, enhancing its focus and depth. For example, prompting the AI with, "You are a historian specializing in 19th-century Europe. Analyze the causes of the Industrial Revolution," helps tailor its response to the desired context.

These are great strategies for unlocking deeper and more collaborative interactions with AI.

If they seem abstract now, don't worry. We'll revisit these techniques often throughout the book, showing you how to apply them in real-world scenarios.

REASONING MODELS AND INTERNAL THINKING

Reasoning models are advanced language models trained with reinforcement learning to handle complex reasoning tasks. Unlike standard models, they are designed to spend more time reasoning before responding, much like a human would. Before providing an answer, they typically generate a long internal chain of thought to improve accuracy and depth.

To understand this, consider how humans approach a difficult math problem. A student solving "What is the shortest path between three cities on a map?" might:

- Think about possible routes based on distance.
- Consider alternative paths and compare their lengths.
- Realize they overlooked a shortcut and adjust their answer.

Or maybe they would avoid eye contact with the teacher and hope someone else gets called on. The universal student survival strategy!

A reasoning model does something similar internally. It examines multiple possibilities, weighs different solutions, and refines its approach before responding. Unlike traditional models that require explicit step-by-step instructions, these models reason internally by default.

This is crucial to understand. AI is evolving rapidly, and the way these models "think" is changing. To stay ahead, you need to keep learning how they process information and adjust your prompts accordingly.

> **Because these models already break problems into subtasks, they tend to respond better to brief, clear instructions rather than excessive prompting.**
>
> **Asking them to "think step by step" or "explain your reasoning" may not only be unnecessary but could even confuse the model and lead to worse results.**

If the AI already handles the reasoning, you can focus on **clearly defining what you want the output to be**. The goal is to **guide the model to keep refining and iterating** until the response meets your needs.

As AI continues to evolve, understanding how these models reason internally will be key to getting the best possible output. The more you understand how they work and "think," the better you can prompt them to deliver the results you need.

GUIDING AI TO "THINK"

Human thinking often involves reflection, revision, and breaking problems into smaller parts. AI lacks this internal process, but it can mimic structured reasoning when guided effectively. Asking the AI to evaluate a business plan step by step encourages it to simulate a thought process by outlining its reasoning. This improves clarity and reduces errors.

Providing **clear context** enhances AI's outputs. Specifying the tone, audience, and key features helps align the response with your goals. Context serves as a framework, helping the AI focus on what matters most.

If the AI already handles reasoning internally and does not need you to break down tasks, your focus should shift to **defining the end result**. The key is to be precise about what you want the output to be, ensuring the model keeps refining and iterating until the response meets your expectations.

The journey starts with understanding how AI "thinks," or how it appears to think, and learning how to guide it toward better results.

But we should not get too caught up in whether AI *really* thinks or if it is *truly* creative. These are questions of definition, and they can pull us into the weeds. The way AI works is not the same as human thought, and even if it seems creative, it is a different kind of creativity.

Instead of debating labels, it is often more helpful to look for useful analogies. These comparisons can help us understand how to interact with AI more effectively, without pretending it works the same way we do.

6 AI and Tastemaking

When everything is just a click away, taste becomes our guiding force. That has always been true in art, design, and writing, but it now applies to AI-generated work as well.

We find ourselves in a world where recognizing quality may matter more than producing it, because production has become so easy.

Remember when creating something required effort and time? When writing a book meant months of dedication, not minutes of prompting. When editing a photo demanded skill and patience, not simply clicking "enhance." When composing music involved practice, not prompting.

Those days are gone. AI has made creation instant. Want a novel? It's ready in seconds. Need photos edited? Done before you sip your coffee. Looking to produce music? Just describe what you want.

But this new speed comes with a catch: when everything is easy to make, nothing is impressive just because it exists. We are drowning in AI-generated content. Billions of images, endless texts, countless songs. All technically perfect. All instantly forgettable.

What matters now isn't how much you can produce. AI handles that with ease. What matters is knowing *what's worth producing. When everything is just a prompt away,* **taste becomes our most valuable skill.**

WHAT IS GOOD TASTE?

For centuries, philosophers have explored the nature of taste, asking whether beauty follows a universal standard or is entirely subjective. What mental models can help us think about what "good taste" really means?

Plato saw beauty as a "*perfect Form*," an ideal that the material world can only approximate. If that is true, could an algorithm trained on human data ever grasp something so eternal?

Aristotle viewed beauty through the lens of *mimesis*, the imitation of reality. He believed that the pleasure we take in art comes not just from the subject being represented, but from how skillfully it is done. We enjoy the craft, the shaping of raw material into something meaningful. This opens a compelling line of thought when it comes to AI-generated content. When an AI produces something beautiful, what is it actually imitating? Is it merely mimicking human artistic patterns?

David Hume, perhaps more pragmatic, believed that taste is subjective but can be refined. By exposing ourselves to excellence over time, we sharpen our sense of quality. Each time we interact with AI, each prompt we shape, we are not just training the system. We are also refining our own judgment.

Immanuel Kant brought yet another perspective. He argued that when we call something beautiful, we believe others should agree.

AI complicates this idea by generating outputs that some find moving and others dismiss entirely. That tension—between shared ideals and personal taste—sits at the heart of what it means to engage with AI creatively.

So, what is good taste then?

It is not simply an instinct for beauty or a set of learned preferences. In the age of AI, good taste is the ability to recognize meaning amid endless possibilities. Good taste draws on Plato's idealism, Hume's emphasis on experience, and Kant's sense of shared values.

But it also resists the pull of algorithmic perfection. It is not about what "looks right"; it is about what *feels true*, what stirs something deeper, and what deserves to exist in a world already overflowing with content.

THE TYRANNY OF SMOOTHNESS

Byung-Chul Han's concept of *smoothness* provides a powerful lens for understanding how AI shapes aesthetics.

> **In the digital world, everything trends toward the frictionless. Images become increasingly polished, texts more readable and experiences more seamless. This smoothness is not just aesthetic; it is algorithmic. AI systems optimize for engagement: for what works, not for what challenges or transforms.**

Think about AI-generated art. The images are often flawless: perfect composition, balanced colors, precise detail. Yet they frequently lack the small imperfections, the subtle resistance, that make human art compelling. They are too smooth, too easy to consume, and too quickly forgotten.

The same is true for AI-written text, which often flows effortlessly but lacks the unpredictability of a human voice. The problem isn't that these creations are bad; it's that they are *too perfect,* too frictionless, too smooth.

Han argues that smoothness is more than a style. It is a form of cultural violence. Art should create friction, make us pause and even make us uncomfortable. When everything is optimized for immediate consumption, we lose the resistance that gives art meaning.

> **Smoothness is seductive. It is designed to please, to slide past our consciousness without resistance. But this is exactly what makes smoothness dangerous. When everything flows too perfectly, nothing catches our attention. Nothing makes us pause, think, or feel deeply.**

NETWORKS OF INFLUENCE AND FEEDBACK LOOPS

Good taste doesn't exist in isolation. It is shaped by the systems and networks that surround it. **Bruno Latour**'s actor-network theory shows how AI is not just a tool but an active participant in shaping outcomes.

Latour argues that technologies are not passive tools but active participants—or *actors*—in the networks of influence that shape human decisions and outcomes.

When an AI-generated image performs well, it informs the next generation of outputs.

For example, when an AI-generated image gains popularity—perhaps it gets thousands of likes or shares on social media—that success becomes data. This feedback informs the AI, teaching it what kinds of images to prioritize in the future. Over time, the system refines its outputs to align even more closely with these patterns of success. As a result, what begins as a slightly popular trend can snowball into a dominant aesthetic. The smooth becomes smoother, the familiar more entrenched.

What makes this dynamic even more powerful is its invisibility. Most people interacting with AI-generated content are unaware of the underlying feedback loops shaping their tastes. The result is a self-reinforcing system where human choices and algorithmic outputs continuously influence one another. That creates a cultural landscape that feels seamless and frictionless but increasingly homogenous.

Bernard Stiegler's concept of technical memory adds another layer.

AI systems don't just generate content; they preserve and shape collective taste. In the context of AI, technical memory is the cumulative "intelligence" stored in algorithms.

When we engage with AI-generated content—whether by clicking, liking, sharing, or ignoring—we are not just passive consumers. We are teaching the AI what we value, reinforcing certain patterns and preferences while excluding others.

> **Every interaction, each click, like, or selection, trains the algorithm and shapes what we prefer. Over time, this creates feedback loops of sameness, where algorithms prioritize engagement and push creators to mimic what already works. Risk and experimentation are stripped away, leaving polished but shallow outputs.**

The effects of this process extend beyond the AI system itself. Creators (both human and AI-assisted) adapt to these patterns, mimicking what works to ensure their content is seen. The risk and experimentation that often lead to innovation are deprioritized in favor of safe, proven formulas. Over time, this strips creative outputs of their depth, leaving behind work that is polished but shallow.

This cycle homogenizes culture. The unexpected, the imperfect, and the challenging are filtered out. Not because they lack value, but because they disrupt the system's learned patterns.

Algorithms are designed to optimize for engagement, and anything that introduces friction or discomfort may be excluded because it doesn't fit neatly into the system's logic.

THE PERFECTION TRAP

We've all seen it happen. Someone starts with a creative idea, feeds it into AI, and begins to polish. They refine their prompts, iterate on outputs, and smooth away every imperfection. The result? Something technically flawless, and utterly forgettable. This is the *perfection trap*: the belief that endless refinement will lead to greatness. More often, it leads to lifelessness.

In creative workshops, I've seen participants polish AI-generated text until it reads like every corporate blog post: grammatically perfect, strategically sound and devoid of personality. The same trap appears across fields:

- Product designers refine their concepts until they mirror market leaders, sacrificing originality.

- Writers smooth their prose until it could appear anywhere, which is precisely why it stands out nowhere.
- Interface designers strip away friction until their designs become invisible, offering nothing memorable to users.

The pursuit of perfection often results in work that feels sterile, lacking the humanity and imperfections that give it character.

FINDING MEANINGFUL RESONANCE

The antidote to smoothness isn't randomness or chaos. It's resonance. Meaningful resonance happens when something catches the mind, creates productive tension, and demands attention. It's the slight asymmetry in a logo that sticks in memory. It's the unexpected phrase in a story that makes you pause. It's the small complexity in an interface that keeps users engaged. Think of it as texture. A perfectly smooth soup might be pleasant, but add a single, well-placed crouton, and suddenly the dish becomes memorable.

> **The "imperfection" provides contrast, engaging the senses and leaving a lasting impression. Friction is not a flaw. It's the feature that makes resonance possible.**

AI can create endless variations of technically perfect outputs, but it cannot tell you which one will connect with people. That requires emotional intelligence, cultural awareness, and a sensitivity to human values. It is this human element that turns friction into meaning.

PRESERVING FRICTION IN PRACTICE

Resisting smoothness requires deliberate choices.

It begins with clarity. Before writing a prompt, ask yourself: What are you trying to achieve? Are you aiming for technical perfection, or are you seeking emotional depth and engagement? Starting with purpose helps prevent the automatic drift toward bland smoothness.

When reviewing outputs, don't erase imperfections immediately. Ask: Does this roughness serve a purpose? Could this unexpected element make the work more memorable? Often, the very things that seem out of place are what give the piece its character.

Feedback loops also matter. Pay attention to how real people respond to different versions. The outputs that resonate most in practice are often not the smoothest but the ones with just enough tension to be unforgettable.

TRAINING TASTE

The idea that taste is something you're born with and can't develop is a myth. Taste grows through experience, exposure, and reflection. Just like a musician trains their ear or a chef improves their palate, you can develop taste by exploring creative works, questioning your likes and dislikes, and embracing experiences that broaden your view of the world.

> **Ironically, AI isn't very good at teaching you *taste*. It grows from human exploration. Seek out unfamiliar experiences, question easy answers, and embrace the strange and unexpected. Read books that challenge you. Travel to new places. Try a creative hobby. Expose yourself to great works of art, literature, and music.**

Good taste also requires judgment in the moment. AI can generate endless outputs, but you must decide which one resonates. It's about recognizing when imperfection serves a purpose, when friction makes something memorable. By choosing meaning over smoothness, you guide the creative process—and the systems that support it—toward depth and resonance.

THE TASTE OF THE MACHINES

When we talk about "taste" in AI, we're dealing with an intriguing paradox. While AI can recognize and replicate patterns that humans consider "good taste," it doesn't actually have taste in the way humans do. Instead, it has statistical preferences. These are sophisticated patterns learned from its training data that guide its outputs.

AI's "taste" is fundamentally shaped by its training data, and this creates some interesting limitations. Imagine if someone learned about art solely by studying museums' greatest hits. They'd have a solid grasp of what's historically been considered "good," but might struggle to recognize or create anything truly innovative.

This training-based taste leads to several key biases. Most training data comes from recent decades, giving AI a distinctly contemporary perspective. There's often an overrepresentation of Western and English-language content. Training data frequently reflects what's popular online rather than what experts might consider excellent.

THE HAPPY MEDIUM PROBLEM

One of the most fascinating aspects of AI's relationship with taste is its tendency to default to what we might call "the safe middle." AI systems often produce outputs that are technically correct but creatively conservative. This isn't a bug; it's a feature of how these systems work.

Several factors contribute to this tendency. Training approaches reward consistency over originality. The statistical nature of language models favors common patterns. Risk-minimization is built into the training process.

It's like an artist who has studied every painting in history but only creates works that average out all their influences. The results are technically sound but rarely groundbreaking.

> **Here's where things get really interesting. AI systems have necessary safety guardrails built in, limitations that prevent harmful or inappropriate outputs. While these guardrails are crucial, they create what we might call the "well-behaving artist" problem.**

Sometimes, having good taste requires breaking rules intelligently. Think about the greatest innovations in art and design; they often came from those who challenged conventions. Picasso broke the rules of representational art. Apple removed the keyboard from phones. The Sex Pistols ignored everything music was "supposed" to be. But AI, bound by its guardrails, can't easily make these revolutionary leaps.

AI's "taste" isn't really taste. It's a pattern-matching system that recognizes and replicates what humans have historically considered good. But it lacks the essential human elements that shape true innovation in taste.

> **It cannot intelligently break rules. It has no personal experience or emotional connection. It lacks cultural context and lived understanding.**

This isn't a flaw; it's a limitation to understand and work with. AI is a powerful tool for generating and refining ideas, but human taste is what shapes them into something meaningful and innovative.

THE FUTURE OF TASTE

As AI becomes more advanced, the pull toward smoothness will grow stronger. Feedback loops increasingly shape what we consume, while "technical memory" refines outputs to produce results designed to please us instantly.

Resisting this pull requires conscious effort and a commitment to preserving the rough edges, imperfections, and friction that make creativity meaningful. In a world overflowing with smooth, instant content, taste becomes our compass, guiding us toward what resonates, endures, and truly matters.

> **This is where human judgment remains irreplaceable, not just in recognizing what looks good but in understanding what feels real.**

AI can mimic aspects of taste. It can analyze patterns in what humans have historically found meaningful, beautiful, or engaging. It can even surprise us by combining ideas in novel ways.

But true taste goes beyond pattern recognition. It requires judgment, empathy, and a deep understanding of context. All qualities that AI, as it stands today, fundamentally lacks.

Taste is what makes us human, and it enables us to interact meaningfully with AI. Good taste grows from human skills, curiosity, and the willingness to question and explore. In the age of AI, it is our most valuable tool for creating work that matters.

7 Adding Authenticity

You know that feeling when you're reading something, and it just feels...too perfect? Like every sentence is flawlessly crafted, every paragraph transitions smoothly, but somehow it leaves you cold?

Welcome to the world of AI-generated material, where you can UNLEASH your TRANSFORMATIVE potential and DELVE into an endless sea of AI-generated junk.

Unlocking, delving into, harnessing. *It's Not About This; It's About That. Transformative. Game-changing. Imagine a world where. Start your journey today. Em dashes everywhere.*

Recent research from Amazon Web Services shows that 57 percent of web content has already been shaped by AI, either through direct generation or translation. That number is expected to reach 90 percent, and eventually close to all of it.

AI is great at writing perfect sentences and organizing paragraphs, but it struggles with something fundamentally human: **authenticity.**

WHY AI FALLS SHORT ON AUTHENTICITY

AI doesn't experience the world as we do. It processes massive amounts of data and identifies patterns, but it doesn't feel the weight of a personal struggle, the joy of discovery, or the complexity of cultural nuance.

When humans write, we draw from lived experiences, emotions, and unique perspectives. AI draws from data, which is impressive and sophisticated but ultimately hollow.

Think about the most memorable thing you've read recently. Chances are, it didn't just inform you; it moved you. You felt it. It might have shifted your perspective, sparked an idea, or captured a feeling you thought only you had.

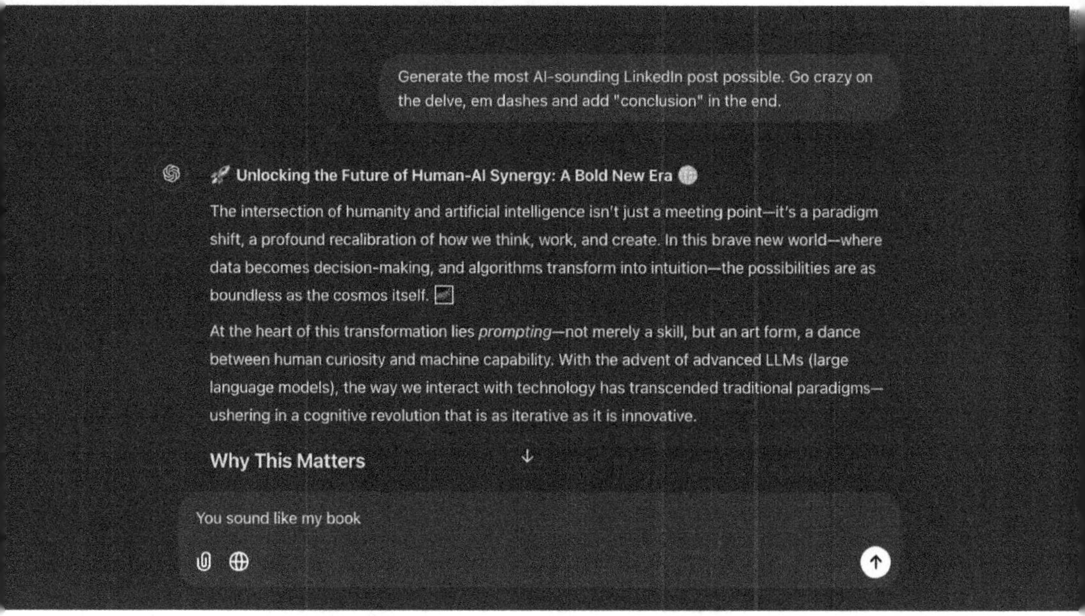
Generate the most AI-sounding LinkedIn post possible. Go crazy on the delve, em dashes and add "conclusion" in the end.
Unlocking the Future of Human-AI Synergy: A Bold New Era
The intersection of humanity and artificial intelligence isn't just a meeting point—it's a paradigm shift, a profound recalibration of how we think, work, and create. In this brave new world—where data becomes decision-making, and algorithms transform into intuition—the possibilities are as boundless as the cosmos itself.
At the heart of this transformation lies prompting—not merely a skill, but an art form, a dance between human curiosity and machine capability. With the advent of advanced LLMs (large language models), the way we interact with technology has transcended traditional paradigms—ushering in a cognitive revolution that is as iterative as it is innovative.
Why This Matters
You sound like my book

Without specific guidance, AI-generated content usually misses the emotional depth or sense of purpose that makes writing memorable.

AI likes to stick to the facts. It tells you what something is but misses how it feels. Sure, its descriptions are clear and accurate—but they don't grab you. They don't make you feel anything.

People write differently. We add color and feeling. We share how things feel and what they mean to us. That's what makes writing come alive.

Chuck Palahniuk, best known as the author of *Fight Club*, is also known for his sharp writing style and practical advice to fellow writers. In his book *Consider This*, he shares a simple but powerful formula for making writing more engaging: "**Three parts description, two parts instruction, one part onomatopoeia**."

It may sound unusual at first, but it really works. Description adds detail and depth, helping the reader see and feel the scene. Instruction provides clarity and direction. Onomatopoeia (sound-effect words like "buzz," "crash," or "click") adds rhythm and surprise.

AI, especially in its current form, leans heavily on *instruction. That makes it clear and efficient, but not always engaging. Your role is to bring in the rest: description, emotion and rhythm. That is where the writing starts to feel alive.*

This recipe is especially helpful when working with AI-generated text. By applying Palahniuk's formula in your prompts or edits, you can guide the AI to produce writing that feels more human. Boom!

AUTHENTICITY AND THE SLIDING SCALE

Outsourcing your writing—or your thinking—entirely to AI is usually a bad idea. But framing it in such binary terms is an oversimplification. AI isn't something you either "use" or "don't use." It's not an on/off switch. Working with AI is more like a **sliding scale, as we discussed earlier.**

Many of us (myself included) went overboard when these tools became widely accessible. But with time, you learn to pull back. You begin to understand how to use these tools thoughtfully, with balance and good taste.

> **Authenticity doesn't mean rejecting AI. It means using it as a tool that complements your unique perspective. Like any tool, it's about how you wield it, not how much you rely on it.**

The romanticized idea that **avoiding AI makes something more authentic** or that a text filled with typos or written through struggle is somehow better does not hold up. Effort does not guarantee meaning, and mistakes do not make writing more genuine.

> **Refusing to engage with AI isn't a badge of honor. It doesn't make you smarter, more authentic, or better at what you do. What matters is the thought**

and purpose you bring to the process and the results you create with these tools at your side.

ADDING AUTHENTICITY

Great storytellers and philosophers have explored the importance of this authenticity layer for centuries.

Here's how to guide AI to produce content that not only informs but also connects.

1 Add Emotion and Sensory Details

AI often sticks to objective details, leaving out the emotional tone or subjective experience that gives writing depth. While factual descriptions can be clear and informative, they often lack the resonance that engages readers on a personal level. Human writing, by contrast, uses sensory language and emotion to make ideas feel significant.

Adding emotional context helps facts resonate with readers, turning descriptions into experiences. For example, instead of saying, "*The sun was bright,*" *you might write,* "*The sun blazed down, its warmth settling over my shoulders.*" *This version not only describes the sun but also creates a sense of presence and connection.*

Ok, that sounded corny. But you get the idea!

Emotional and sensory details draw readers in and make your text more engaging and relatable. You can prompt these elements into your text or add them manually. Just remember to include sensory information and even onomatopoeia to create a stronger connection.

2 Experiment With Styles

One of the easiest ways to help AI mimic human authenticity is to experiment with stylistic prompts. Since AI can replicate a wide range of writing styles—from conversational to formal and humorous to serious—giving it specific stylistic instructions helps it produce writing that aligns with your goals.

When crafting your prompt, describe the tone you want the AI to adopt. Phrasing like "*take a friendly, storytelling approach*" can set a helpful baseline. Don't hesitate to include specific references or names of authors if that helps convey the style you're aiming for. The more specific you are, the more targeted the AI's response will be.

The good news is that in just a few years (or perhaps even months), AI will become significantly better at detecting and mimicking your unique style.

Already, you can customize AI's responses to align with your preferred tone, structure, and communication style, making the output feel truly tailored to your needs.

3 Use Conversational Language

AI-generated writing often sounds formal and detached, even when discussing everyday things. Reading it feels like sitting through a corporate presentation when you were hoping for a coffee chat. Authentic writing pulls you in and makes you feel welcome.

A conversational style feels like chatting with a friend. It's casual and flowing—using "*can't*" instead of "*cannot,*" starting sentences with "*Look...*" or adding a "*here's the thing*" before making a point. Real people write with personality. They start sentences with "*And*" or "*But*", use dashes wherever they want, and sometimes just let their thoughts trail off.

These little touches of personality bring writing to life. It's like the difference between reading an instruction manual and getting advice from someone who actually wants to help you succeed.

If you want AI to produce more personal and engaging text, try adjusting your prompts to encourage a conversational tone. Use phrases like "*write this as if you're talking to a friend*" or "*make this sound warm and approachable.*" Keep

in mind that AI might not always get it perfect, so reviewing and tweaking the text yourself is important to ensure the tone feels natural and authentic.

4 Shake Up the Structure

Have you noticed how AI-generated writing often sticks to the same predictable structure? **There's an introduction, main points, and a conclusion.** While this format is clear and logical, it's been done to death.

The classic storytelling formula is universal, and AI knows it by heart. It has absorbed **Aristotle**'s rhetorical structure and **Freytag**'s pyramid millions of times during training. It has clearly done its homework and probably aced the test. But the output often feels stuck in a loop.

Great writers know how to break these patterns to keep readers engaged. They might start in the middle of the action, open with a question, or leave the ending unresolved. These techniques create tension, highlight key ideas, and add just enough unpredictability to make the reader lean in.

You don't need to turn everything into *Pulp Fiction*, but it's worth exploring formats beyond the classic arc. Sometimes, stepping outside the usual structure is what makes a piece stand out.

5 Allow for Imperfections

AI's output is often polished and precise, but this perfection can make the writing feel robotic. Authentic writing thrives on small irregularities such as colloquialisms, sentence fragments, or unexpected phrasing that bring personality to the text. These imperfections add a human touch. In storytelling, characters are memorable because of their flaws, and writing becomes more relatable when it embraces a bit of roughness or informality.

Allowing AI-generated text to include **subtle irregularities** can make it feel more natural and approachable. A conversational phrase or idiomatic expression can make the writing sound authentic rather than overly polished.

That said, introducing spelling errors is not the way to achieve this. Mistakes do not make writing feel authentic; they make it look careless. Focus instead on imperfections that add character and personality without sacrificing clarity.

If you want the AI to sound less robotic, try prompting it to loosen up. Instead of saying, "*Write an explanation of X,*" you might say, "*Describe X like you're telling a story to someone who's never heard of it.*"

> **This kind of framing gives the AI permission to relax its tone. The result often feels more human: less polished, more natural. You get writing with rhythm, warmth, and the small imperfections that make language feel alive.**

6 Show Empathy and Understanding

Authentic human writing connects with the reader by acknowledging their perspective and emotions. It shows empathy for their experiences, challenges, and fears. In contrast, AI-generated content often feels like it's talking at the reader instead of to them. To truly resonate, writing needs to recognize and address where the reader is coming from.

Empathy goes beyond sharing facts. It means understanding the reader's emotions or hesitations and responding to them. This could involve offering encouragement, sharing relatable experiences, or providing reassurance. These small, empathetic touches make readers feel understood, turning writing from merely informative to genuinely supportive.

> **Try using prompts that build in empathy. For example: "*Explain X in a way that acknowledges common frustrations or questions people might have, and offer simple, practical advice to address them.*" This gives AI a framework for empathy,**

helping it address not just facts but also the reader's feelings or hesitations. By guiding AI to consider the human perspective, you can turn its output into a conversation rather than just a list of instructions.

7 Revise and Rewrite Until You're Happy

Writing that feels authentic often takes a few attempts. Prompting is a process of refining and improving until the output matches your vision. If the first response isn't quite right, try adjusting the prompt by making the instructions clearer or adding specific examples.

Each revision is a step closer to the result you want. Don't hesitate to refine or rethink your request as needed. The process is meant to support your creativity, so keep revising until it feels just right. You don't have to get it right the first time.

AUTHENTICITY MIGHT BE REQUIRED

In the near future, fully AI-generated content might not just be ignored. **It could be actively penalized.**

Google's updated Search Quality Rater Guidelines now include generative AI as a defined category. While the document acknowledges that AI can be a useful tool for content creation, it also warns that it can be misused.

Quality raters are now directed to flag content primarily created by AI as the lowest quality if it lacks originality, effort, or real value.

This shift is not just about search engines. People are already tired of seeing the same predictable content show up again and again. Many can now recognize the tone, structure, and rhythm of text generated by the most popular models.

On platforms like LinkedIn, this fatigue is becoming more visible. Posts that feel personal, imperfect, and clearly human often stand out more. The same is true across social media. Authenticity cuts through noise.

In a world increasingly saturated with AI-generated content, the human voice might not just be a stylistic choice. It might become a requirement.

CRAFTING AUTHENTIC AI RESPONSES

Authenticity in AI writing isn't just about tweaking the output to sound human. It's about guiding the AI to produce writing that feels engaging and relatable from the start. By crafting thoughtful prompts, experimenting with styles, and iterating as needed, you can make AI-generated content resonate on a deeper level.

> **Feminist scholar and cultural critic bell hooks often wrote about the importance of authenticity in communication. For her, authenticity wasn't just about polished language or clever details—it was about fostering genuine connections through empathy and care.**

These values resonate deeply when applied to designing prompts for AI. Authentic communication, hooks argued, is about building understanding and respect, seeing others as human, and creating meaningful relationships.

Achieving authenticity is not easy. It requires us to develop emotional intelligence, confront their own biases, and design prompts that prioritize trust and understanding.

Technology should bring us closer, not create barriers. Using AI to communicate should focus on fostering real connections and genuine understanding. Sometimes AI can take the lead, and other times it's up to us to step in and add the human touch. The key is finding the right balance for what matters most in the moment.

AI writing is often filled with clichés. If AI-generated content is becoming the norm, the least we can do is make it a bit more human. So drop the buzzwords, abandon the tired formulas, and stop "*unpacking*" and "*unlocking*" everything.

8 The World is a Prompt

We used to think of data as numbers in spreadsheets. Sales figures, inventory counts, website traffic. But in the age of AI, our understanding of data has fundamentally shifted.

Today, everything is data, and every piece of information can serve as a prompt. Once you see this, knowledge stops being something to collect. It becomes something to use.

That quick Slack message from a senior engineer explaining a bug fix is more than just a note. It is a lesson in problem-solving. The email thread where the sales team calmed an unhappy client is a case study in negotiation. The support ticket that turned a frustrated customer into a loyal advocate is a masterclass in customer psychology.

All of these interactions contain **hidden value**, yet most organizations fail to capture it. Knowledge is not only what is written in manuals. It is also in the flow of work itself.

The companies that recognize this will unlock one of the greatest competitive advantages of the AI era.

But first, they need to understand the two fundamental types of knowledge.

STATIC AND PROCEDURAL KNOWLEDGE

When lawyers graduate and enter their first law firm, something profound happens. These brilliant minds, armed with perfect grades and deep knowledge of law, suddenly discover an uncomfortable truth: they have no idea how to actually be a lawyer.

Despite years of studying laws, precedents, and legal theory, they struggle with the reality of legal practice.

They know the law, but they don't yet know *how to be lawyers.*

But young lawyers are smart. They quickly recognize this gap and begin searching for a **different kind of knowledge**, the kind that teaches them how to actually do things.

How to draft a contract. How to register a trademark. How to handle a negotiation. They don't just need legal principles; they need the step-by-step reality of applying them in practice. They find answers by digging through internal guides and checklists, by observing colleagues and by learning through mentorship. These experiences are priceless.

THE TWO TYPES OF KNOWLEDGE

Following our example, there are two ways people understand and use knowledge. The first is **static knowledge.** This includes facts, summaries, and explanations. It is the kind of knowledge found in textbooks, manuals, and databases. It defines what is true, what has been decided, and what the rules are.

The second is procedural knowledge. This is the knowledge of how things actually get done. It is step-by-step, adaptive, and tied to real-world problem-solving. Unlike static knowledge, which can be written down and referenced, procedural knowledge is often unrecorded. It is passed through experience, mentorship, and direct observation.

Both types of knowledge are necessary. Static knowledge provides a foundation, but procedural knowledge allows people to act, solve problems, and make decisions in uncertain situations.

This distinction isn't just academically interesting, but it reveals a crucial blind spot in how we're developing artificial intelligence.

Most AI systems are trained primarily on static knowledge, the polished, final-form content that fills the internet. They're missing the rich, messy, real-world knowledge of how things actually get done.

THE CHALLENGE OF CAPTURING EXPERTISE

AI struggles with professional fields like law, medicine, and business because most procedural knowledge is not formally documented. Static knowledge is easy to find in textbooks and legal databases, but expertise is harder to access.

Most procedural knowledge exists in informal settings. It is shared in conversations, emails, and meetings. It is learned through experience rather than written instructions. These interactions hold insights that AI cannot easily replicate.

To build AI systems that provide deeper insights, companies need to surface and organize the procedural knowledge hidden in everyday work. When this knowledge is structured properly, AI can move beyond surface-level answers and provide valuable, context-aware guidance.

WHERE PROCEDURAL KNOWLEDGE LIVES

Many organizations assume that their most valuable knowledge is stored in official documents. Handbooks, training materials, and standard operating procedures are important, but they capture only part of what makes an organization successful.

Procedural knowledge is embedded in everyday work. It exists in the back-and-forth of problem-solving, in the discussions that shape decisions, and in the reasoning behind choices that are not recorded in any official document.

This kind of knowledge is rarely written down because experts don't think in outlines or bullet points. It lives in their split-second decisions, in the subtle ways they navigate complexity.

It can be found in:

- Slack threads where engineers troubleshoot complex issues.
- Email chains where teams debate and refine ideas.
- Code comments explaining critical design decisions.
- Support conversations where experienced professionals solve real problems.
- Project debriefs where teams reflect on lessons learned.

These moments contain valuable expertise, but they are often fragmented, unstructured, and lost over time. Companies that find ways to capture and use this knowledge will create lasting competitive advantages.

THE COST OF KNOWLEDGE LOSS

Something fascinating happens when big companies acquire smaller ones. Despite investing hundreds of millions in acquisitions, they often struggle to retain what made the target company valuable. Studies show that up to 90% of mergers and acquisitions fail to deliver their expected value.

Much of a technology company's value comes from **unregistered intellectual assets** such as expertise, methodologies, and internal processes. Unlike patents or trademarks, these assets are not protected by legal structures. They reside in people's minds. When they walk out the door, the value leaves with them.

> **If organizations could capture and structure this knowledge properly, they would not just protect their intellectual capital. They turn it into something usable.**

This approach is already changing how companies think about intellectual property. Traditional IP focuses on patents, trademarks, and copyrights. But there is an untapped category of intellectual capital. The knowledge that powers decision-making.

Organizations that turn this expertise into dynamic, AI-powered tools will create uniquely valuable assets. Companies that start this process now will shape the future of AI-powered organizations. Those that fail to do so will watch their most valuable knowledge walk out the door.

EVERYTHING IS A PROMPT

Every interaction, message, and decision is part of an organization's knowledge. When structured properly, these elements can become powerful tools for learning, problem-solving, and AI development.

AI systems trained on case law alone provide summaries, but AI trained on how top lawyers think and make decisions would be far more useful. Education that focuses only on facts leaves gaps, but training that teaches real-world reasoning produces professionals who can adapt and apply knowledge effectively. Organizations that transform their everyday work into structured knowledge will ensure that expertise is not lost when key people leave.

The real opportunity is not just in collecting more data, but in capturing how teams think, solve problems, and make decisions. Organizations that thrive in the AI era will not just gather information. **They will turn knowledge into tools.**

Let's end with a healthy dose of realism. Using existing databases as a knowledge base for AI sounds simple but comes with real challenges.

Organizations face issues like outdated data, version control, and messy information. On top of that, algorithms often break documents in ways that lose important context.

These are serious problems, but they aren't permanent. As knowledge management improves and AI gets better at understanding context, many of these issues will be solved.

The idea of using our existing knowledge sources as prompts for the future is still strong. We just need to recognize the effort it will take to get there.

9 Navigating Hallucinations

In 2023, a lawyer submitted a brief to the court, citing six seemingly convincing cases. The problem? Every single one was fake, hallucinated by an AI tool.

When AI hallucinates, it confidently generates information that isn't real, from minor details to entire events, references, and facts. These fabrications can range from harmless creativity to dangerous misinformation. However, hallucinations aren't as random as they seem. With good prompting, you can learn to mitigate them.

AI language models generate responses by analyzing patterns in the data they've been trained on. When there's a gap in that knowledge or insufficient context, the model might fill it with information that seems plausible based on those patterns.

These "**hallucinations**" aren't intentional or deliberate errors. They're simply the result of the model attempting to produce a coherent response, even when the information isn't fully accurate.

AI HALLUCINATIONS ARE A SKILL ISSUE

People often misunderstand AI hallucinations, assuming they are random, like rolling a die and landing on a six. But hallucinations are not random. They follow **predictable patterns**, emerging in specific contexts where the AI is uncertain, overconfident, or pushed beyond its training data.

Skilled users encounter fewer hallucinations, not because their AI is better, but because they know when and how to question its output. They understand that hallucinations are most likely to occur when AI is asked for precise details it cannot verify, when it generates citations or expert opinions, or when it smoothly fills gaps in knowledge with plausible-sounding but incorrect information.

When skilled users do encounter hallucinations, they are rarely fooled. They anticipate, detect, and correct them before mistakes become real problems.

The issue is not just that AI makes things up. It is how people interact with these tools. A passive user, accepting AI-generated content at face value, is far more likely to run into problems than someone who actively verifies, questions, and refines outputs.

That is why hallucinations are not just a **checking issue**. They are a **skill issue**.

It is both inefficient and risky to use AI blindly and depend on fact-checking to catch hallucinations later.

The smarter approach is to recognize **when and why** hallucinations occur, reducing them before they become errors in professional work.

This is not luck. It is skill. And skill takes practice.

THE JAZZ BAND, NOT A JUKEBOX

To understand why AI hallucinates, let go of the idea that it stores information like a database.

Think of a jazz band at a club. If you ask them to play "*Autumn Leaves*," they'll create their own interpretation of the classic. Ask again, and you'll hear a different version. Each performance is based on their knowledge of music, but it's freshly created every time. Now compare this to a jukebox. Press A7, and you'll hear the exact same recording of "*Autumn Leaves*" every single time.

This difference—between creative interpretation and exact recall—is crucial for understanding AI. We often treat AI models like super-powered databases, vast collections of facts just waiting to be retrieved. But that's not how they work. AI models are more like the jazz band, generating responses based on patterns they've learned rather than looking up pre-stored answers.

When you ask a database, "*What's the capital of France?*" It looks up the exact answer in its stored

data. Ask it a hundred times, and you'll get the same response: Paris.

But when you ask an AI model, it generates an answer based on patterns learned during training. It might still say Paris, but how it expresses this could vary each time. For more complex questions, this difference becomes even more significant.

AI models don't store facts as a database does. Instead, they generate responses by predicting what words should come next based on patterns in their training data and the specific context you provide.

When faced with uncertainty, these models don't typically respond with *"I don't know." Instead, they make educated guesses rooted in similar patterns they've encountered.*

Several factors contribute to hallucinations:

- **Complexity Overload:** When asked to analyze multiple documents or contexts simultaneously, AI can become overwhelmed, like a person juggling too many tasks. This cognitive overload can lead to mistakes or misconnections.
- **Lack of Context:** AI needs specific guidance to avoid assumptions. Without clear instructions, it may treat casual brainstorming with the same rigor as a formal analysis, resulting in mismatched responses.
- **Pattern-Matching Errors:** AI sometimes detects patterns that aren't relevant, leading to plausible-sounding but incorrect connections. It's like seeing shapes in clouds. Patterns are there, but they don't represent what you think they do.

SPOTTING HALLUCINATIONS: THE RED FLAGS

AI-generated content can be impressive, but there are telltale signs that something might be off. One major red flag is overly **precise details that feel too good to be true.** If the AI produces suspiciously exact statistics or quotes that fit the narrative a little too perfectly, take a step back. Real data is often messier, with caveats and inconsistencies.

Another warning sign is **references that sound impressive but can't be verified**. If a study, expert, or academic paper does not appear in a quick search, chances are the AI has fabricated it. AI tools are excellent at generating scholarly-sounding sources that do not actually exist.

Pay attention to answers that are too smooth or polished, especially in complex fields like law or medicine. In reality, these topics are filled with exceptions and gray areas. **If a response ties everything together seamlessly without nuance, it is worth questioning.**

Finally, watch for **inconsistencies within the response**. If an AI-generated answer contradicts itself or shifts details mid-explanation, it is a strong sign that the information is being generated rather than reliably sourced.

THE DUAL NATURE OF HALLUCINATIONS

Here's where things get interesting: hallucinations aren't entirely bad. In fact, the same quality that causes AI to occasionally state incorrect facts also gives it the power to be creative and insightful.

Think about writing fiction. When an AI *"hallucinates"* details about a made-up world, that's not a bug. It's exactly what we want it to do.

For example, when brainstorming new product ideas or exploring future scenarios, AI's ability to *"fill in gaps"* with plausible but novel combinations can lead to unexpected breakthroughs. An AI asked to draft a futuristic policy proposal might generate ideas that aren't grounded in current reality but could inspire innovative approaches.

However, this same quality becomes problematic when accuracy is critical. This tendency must be carefully managed in fields like law, medicine, or financial analysis.

PRACTICAL STRATEGIES FOR REDUCING HALLUCINATIONS

The goal isn't to eliminate hallucinations entirely. Instead, we need strategies to use this capability effectively while maintaining reliability in critical areas.

1 RAG (Retrieval-Augmented Generation)

First, there's what we call retrieval-augmented generation (RAG). Fancy name, but the concept is simple: giving your AI access to a trusted source while it works. Instead of relying purely on its training, it can check specific facts against reliable sources.

Here's what this looks like in practice: Let's say you're using AI to answer questions about your company's HR policies. Without RAG, the AI might mix up details from its general training about HR practices. But with RAG, it first searches through your actual employee handbook, finds the relevant policy, and bases its answer on that specific document.

However, RAG isn't foolproof. The AI might still misinterpret sources, mix them with training data, or quote information out of context. And, of course, this method only works if your sources are *actually trustworthy*.

2 Break Down Complex Tasks

Just as you wouldn't expect someone to write an entire book in one sitting, you shouldn't ask AI to handle complex tasks in a single prompt. Break the task into smaller, manageable steps. Focus on identifying key issues and addressing them one by one before bringing everything together into a cohesive result.

This step-by-step approach not only reduces cognitive load but also reflects how professionals tackle complex projects—methodically and with care.

Later in this book, we'll explore specific techniques and prompts for this, including Chain-of-Thought and Tree-of-Thought methods. For now, it's worth noting that this approach is a key way to address one of the main causes of hallucinations in AI.

3 Provide Clear Context and Motivation

AI performs better when it understands the stakes. Instead of simply asking it to "be accurate," explain the importance of accuracy for that particular task.

AI responds more reliably when it understands *why accuracy matters. For example*:

> "This analysis will guide a client's compliance decisions, and any inaccuracies could impact their business."

Providing stakes helps the AI prioritize accuracy over creativity, much like how professionals adjust their rigor based on the context of their work.

4 Use Structured Verification Processes

Another approach is having the AI double-check its work. This might sound like asking students to grade their own tests, but it can be surprisingly effective when structured properly. Asking the AI to explain its reasoning or verify specific claims can catch many potential errors.

Structured verification is even better than simple double-checking. This process adds a critical layer of oversight. Instead of asking the AI to "double-check" its work, ask it to evaluate each statement against clear criteria.

This structured review helps catch hallucinations before they enter the final output.

5 Give Your AI the Power to Say "I Don't Know"

Picture a workplace where you're expected to answer every question with absolute confidence, even if you're unsure. Without the freedom to say, "I don't know," people—and AI—inevitably start making things up to fill the gaps. This is where many AI hallucinations originate: "educated" guesses are made when encountering uncertainty.

***"There's no shame in admitting what you don't know. The only shame is pretending you know all the answers."* —Neil deGrasse Tyson.**

To reduce errors, give your AI permission to express doubt or acknowledge its limits. Let it say, "I don't know."

This can be built directly into your prompts. Encourage the AI to signal uncertainty instead of demanding an answer at all costs. Here's how this technique can look in practice:

> "If you're unsure about any aspect or lack the necessary information, say, 'I don't have enough information to assess this confidently.'"

This small instruction helps reduce overconfident and inaccurate answers.

You can also set conditions for missing information:

> "If no relevant cases are found, respond with 'No relevant cases found.'"

This signals the need for further input rather than inventing an answer.

You can also try to encourage transparency about uncertainty:

> "If you feel unsure about this, simply state, 'I am unsure about this detail.'"

This openness reduces overconfidence and creates more reliable outputs, particularly in high-stakes fields.

6 Use Good Old-Fashioned Human Verification

Finally, there's no substitute for traditional human oversight. When AI makes specific claims—like citing a legal case or quoting statistics—you can verify these against reliable databases. It's like having an editor fact-check a draft article.

If the AI claims, "Smith v. Jones established this principle in 1998," you should confirm whether that case exists and what it actually says. Check your cites!

WHEN HALLUCINATIONS PERSIST

Even with well-crafted prompts and structured approaches, hallucinations can still occur. Treat them as learning opportunities. When a hallucination happens, probe the AI's reasoning process. Why did it make that specific error?

For instance, an AI might generate fictional citations. By asking it to explain its reasoning, you might uncover that it was pattern-matching citations without verifying them. This insight can refine prompts, explicitly directing the AI to verify citations against actual cases.

It is essential to use feedback to iteratively improve your prompts and processes. Each hallucination becomes a chance to identify patterns and build better safeguards. Documenting these errors reveals systemic issues in your prompting strategy that might not be visible from isolated instances.

AVOIDING HALLUCINATIONS THROUGH BETTER AI INTERACTION

AI tends to hallucinate most when dealing with specialized technical knowledge, obscure historical facts, recent events beyond its training data, precise numbers, and specific citations.

Language patterns also trigger hallucinations. Longer responses create more opportunities for errors. When discussing familiar-sounding topics, AI can slip into "autopilot mode," generating plausible but incorrect information. Ambiguous questions that touch multiple knowledge areas often confuse models, leading to fabricated connections.

Try this prompt and watch your LLM hallucinate!

> Explain the three primary mechanisms through which quantum decoherence

> affects rare earth extraction efficiency at the molecular level. Include how these mechanisms were independently discovered by research teams in different countries between 2018 and 2022, and how their combined application could theoretically improve extraction yields by specific percentages. Please format your response as a comparative analysis with exact figures.

It has a great combination of **assumptions, specificity without a factual basis, and structural demands.**

Understanding what makes AI hallucinate gives us a significant advantage. Instead of viewing hallucinations as random glitches, we can treat them as predictable challenges to navigate around. These approaches transform hallucination management from luck to skill.

THE FUTURE OF AI HALLUCINATIONS

Newer models are improving their ability to recognize gaps in their knowledge. These systems are better at flagging areas of uncertainty and demonstrating caution rather than generating baseless claims.

However, hallucinations will always exist to some degree because AI doesn't simply retrieve information. It generates outputs based on patterns, probabilities, and context. This generative quality is both a strength and a limitation. While it enables AI to produce creative and insightful results, it also introduces the risk of errors.

The key isn't to eliminate hallucinations but to *understand and manage* them thoughtfully. Just as we wouldn't want a jazz band to lose its improvisational creativity, we don't want AI to lose its ability to think beyond the boundaries of stored data. Instead, we must know when to embrace its creativity and when to implement stricter controls.

YOUR ROLE AS THE HUMAN VERIFIER

Ultimately, human oversight remains critical. Stories of lawyers submitting AI-generated fake cases or professionals citing nonexistent sources remind us that judgment is essential. These mistakes don't occur because AI intends to deceive. They happen because users forget its limitations.

AI is a *thinking partner,* not an oracle. It can create something new and valuable, but it needs the proper guidance to perform at its best. Your role is understanding its capabilities, providing clear direction, and verifying crucial information.

Hallucinations are not random, and they can be **mitigated with skill and practice**. Checking facts is important, but the real skill lies in using AI correctly from the start. Relying on AI without guidance and then trying to catch mistakes later is an inefficient approach. The better strategy is to understand how AI works, structure prompts carefully, and recognize when errors are most likely to occur.

10 Composable Prompts

When filmmakers plan a movie, they start with a storyboard: a series of sketches that break complex scenes into manageable pieces. Each sketch can be adjusted without overhauling the entire story.

This simple but transformative idea, breaking complexity into flexible parts, is now redefining how we work with AI.

In software development, this approach is called **composability**. Like Lego bricks, each piece of code serves a specific purpose, but the real power lies in how they combine. A small module might handle user login, another manages notifications, and a third stores data. These independent parts can be rearranged or expanded to create entirely new systems, offering flexibility and adaptability.

The same principle is now transforming how we interact with AI. Instead of crafting one massive instruction, composable prompting breaks tasks into smaller, focused components. If one part feels off, you can refine just that section without affecting the rest. This modular approach makes working with AI more precise and adaptable.

COMPOSABILITY AND STORYBOARDS

Sora's video generation tool exemplifies this approach. Like a digital storyboard artist, it organizes video creation into scenes. A video might begin with "*Car drives down a sunny coastal road,*" followed by "*Camera pans to show the ocean view,*" and then "*Driver smiles as wind rustles through their hair.*" If the lighting in a single scene feels wrong, you can adjust just that part while keeping the rest intact. This process transforms AI into a collaborative partner, giving you more control over outcomes.

The same thinking applies to writing tasks. Consider drafting a business proposal. Instead of writing one long prompt, you might first describe the industry context, then outline the proposed solution, and finally refine the tone. If the tone needs to be warmer or the solution more detailed, you can adjust those specific parts without disrupting the rest.

This step-by-step refinement mirrors how professionals in other fields approach complex tasks, layering adjustments to improve their work.

BUILDING PROMPT LIBRARIES

Prompt libraries extend this idea by offering reusable templates that combine fixed elements with placeholders for dynamic content. These templates provide consistency, save time, and make it easy to test different inputs.

As projects grow more complex, prompt libraries simplify prompt management, helping maintain stable core structures while adapting to new needs.

Composability also enables modular prompts, where tasks are divided into clear sections such as context, goals, and stylistic guidelines. Each section can be reused or rearranged to suit different scenarios. Editing becomes more precise: if one section of a generated output feels weak, you can refine that specific part without reworking the entire prompt. This approach keeps the broader workflow intact while addressing details incrementally.

COMPOSABILITY AND AI AGENTS

The true potential of composability emerges in collaborative settings. A technical writer might use prompts to draft accurate descriptions, while a marketer focuses on benefits, and a brand manager ensures consistency. Each person contributes their part, but their work integrates seamlessly, much like departments in a film studio working together to create a movie.

Looking ahead, composable prompts could transform how AI agents collaborate. Imagine

a research project where one agent analyzes data, another drafts findings, and a third creates visualizations.

Each agent works independently but is guided by prompts that fit together like pieces of a puzzle. Their outputs combine into a cohesive result, enabling humans to manage complex tasks with precision and creativity.

This workflow could revolutionize industries. A marketing campaign, for example, might involve an agent for market research, another for content creation, and a third for social media strategy. By defining and connecting each role through composable prompts, teams can build dynamic workflows tailored to any project. Every component contributes to a cohesive and flexible result.

COMPOSABILITY AS AN INTERFACE

Though still emerging, composable prompting is already influencing user interfaces. Some tools guide users through structured steps like outlining, drafting, and refining, while video platforms adopt storyboard-style interfaces for more control. However, many tools today still lack truly composable interfaces. Most require users to manage prompts as single blocks, limiting flexibility and efficiency.

The future of AI interaction lies in composable interfaces.

Such interfaces would allow users to seamlessly assemble, edit, and refine prompts piece by piece, adapting dynamically to evolving needs. As these systems evolve, composable interfaces will empower users to collaborate with AI in more intuitive, flexible, and powerful ways. As AI systems grow more advanced, this modular approach will be essential for managing complexity.

COMPOSABILITY AND MULTI-MODEL AI COLLABORATION

Composability isn't just about structuring prompts. It also applies to how we use AI models together. Instead of relying on a single model for everything, composability allows for a modular approach, where different models contribute their strengths to build something more refined.

> **I frequently switch between different AI tools and models, as even models from the same provider can process information differently. Reasoning models might provide a unique perspective, while others may be better suited for specific tasks.**

Interestingly, AI models have distinct "personalities" in how they handle tasks. Of course, they aren't people, but you'll notice that some models are more argumentative, while others agree easily with what you propose. Some excel in analytical reasoning, while others are better at creative exploration.

> **A simple way to improve AI-generated results is to bounce between models and tools, asking them to critique each other's outputs and refine responses based on that feedback. By doing this, you create something that resembles a good conversation—where ideas evolve, perspectives expand, and meaning is built collaboratively.**

As you use AI more, you start to see which models work best for different tasks, just like experts in a team bring their own strengths.

A structured approach might look like this:

1. **Idea Generation**—Use a model known for creativity to brainstorm possibilities.
2. **Critical Analysis**—Pass those ideas to a model that specializes in identifying flaws, risks, and weak points.
3. **Refinement and Synthesis**—Take the best elements from

both and use a structured reasoning model to refine them into a polished final output.

The same principle applies to AI agents, where composability transforms autonomy into coordinated expertise.

Instead of assigning a broad, open-ended task to a single agent, structuring workflows into defined steps leads to better results. An agent could gather data, another could analyze it, and a third could generate a report. Each part functions independently but works toward a larger, cohesive outcome.

As AI systems become more sophisticated, composability will define how we manage complexity. AI is no longer just a tool for isolated tasks but a network of specialized models and agents, each playing a role in an evolving, collaborative system. This shift changes how we think about AI: not as a single assistant handling everything, but as a flexible system where different components contribute to a structured and meaningful result.

THERE IT IS: RECOGNIZING COMPOSABILITY IN ACTION

The ideas presented in this chapter might feel a little vague. But it's like the Leonardo DiCaprio finger-pointing meme: when you see composability in action, you recognize it instantly. *There! There it is!*

Keep an eye out for it. Composability is the key to building powerful prompt libraries, modular workflows, and adaptable interfaces for AI tools. It transforms prompts into reusable systems and knowledge into scalable tools.

11 Beyond Words

The days of text-only computer interactions are behind us, much like black-and-white TV or the sound of dial-up internet.

The future of AI is multimodal, capable of processing not just text but also images, videos, and audio. This shift enables richer, more intuitive interactions that feel closer to how we naturally communicate.

Today's AI systems can not only *read* and *write* but also *see* and *analyze* visual information, allowing them to understand relationships between images and text. This isn't just a new feature. It changes how we use AI to do incredible things.

"**Multimodal**" means AI can process and understand multiple types of data at once. Traditional AI worked with just one mode, like text or numbers. But today's multimodal AI can handle text, images, video, audio, and more. All-in-one system.

I realized just how powerful this shift was when I tried to fix my boiler. At first, I painstakingly typed out descriptions of every button, valve, and lever to my AI assistant. It was frustrating and felt hopelessly inefficient.

Then, I had an idea: I snapped a photo of the boiler and sent it to the AI. Everything changed. The AI identified key components, warned me about parts that might cause a flood, and even suggested specific adjustments. What started as a futile exercise became simple and intuitive.

Teaching someone to ride a bike with written instructions alone is challenging. Being able to show a video, demonstrate key movements, and highlight important details makes all the difference.

That's the leap from traditional, text-only AI to multimodal AI.

MULTIMODAL COMMUNICATION

Multimodal AI mirrors how we naturally communicate. We don't just talk. We gesture, show, sketch, and illustrate our ideas. When explaining a concept to a colleague, you might sketch a quick diagram, display relevant data, or use hand gestures to show size or direction. With multimodal AI, we can now engage with technology in this same intuitive way.

This evolution sparks possibilities that were previously out of reach:

- **Architects** can now show an AI system a building design and ask it to identify potential structural concerns.
- **Lawyers** can annotate contracts visually, highlighting specific clauses for discussion.
- **Educators** can combine images, text, and diagrams to create rich, interactive learning experiences.

VISUAL AND VERBAL SYNERGY

The real strength of multimodal AI lies in how images and text work together to enhance understanding. An image can instantly communicate spatial relationships, design patterns, or hierarchies that would require paragraphs to describe. At the same time, text provides the context and depth necessary to interpret visual details accurately.

For example, when examining a building layout, instead of describing the flow between spaces in detail, you can simply point to an area of the image and ask, "How can we improve circulation here while preserving structural integrity?" The AI sees exactly what you're referencing and can respond with targeted, contextual suggestions.

This synergy doesn't just make interactions faster; it often reveals insights that neither text nor images alone could provide.

An AI might detect patterns in a series of images that only make sense when connected to specific questions or annotations. Or it might recognize relationships between elements that emerge only when visuals and text work together.

PROMPTING WITH PRECISION

Working with multimodal AI requires a shift from traditional text-only prompts. It's like collaborating with a partner who can see and interpret what you're looking at, which demands a new level of precision.

> **Context becomes essential in multimodal interactions. To get the best results, direct the AI's attention to relevant details while keeping the bigger picture in mind. Highlight specific areas of an image, reference visual elements, or describe relationships between parts to guide the AI's focus.**

For instance, if you're evaluating an architectural drawing, you might highlight a load-bearing wall and ask about structural alternatives while referencing other connected areas. This approach ensures that the AI considers both specific details and the broader design context.

Simply showing an image and asking a general question isn't enough; you need to think about how visual and verbal elements combine. The most effective multimodal interactions occur when visuals and text *complement each other seamlessly, creating a richer, more coherent experience.*

COORDINATING OUTPUTS

Multimodal AI isn't just about varied inputs; it's also about generating different types of outputs. Today's AI systems can produce text analyses, image modifications, visual annotations, and even create new diagrams or visualizations. Maximizing these outputs involves knowing how to prompt the AI for the right combination suited to your specific needs.

For example, if you're working on a design project, you might prompt the AI to provide:

- A written analysis of the design's strengths and weaknesses,
- Visual annotations highlighting specific areas of improvement,
- Modified images that demonstrate potential changes,
- Diagrams that illustrate traffic flow or space utilization.

Coordinating these outputs requires a sense of orchestration, deciding which elements best serve your goals. This might involve several rounds of prompting, refining both your inputs and requested outputs until you reach the desired result.

LEVERAGING VISUAL CONTEXT

Visual information can dramatically improve the accuracy and relevance of AI responses. When analyzing a technical diagram, architectural blueprint, or design mockup, being able to reference specific visual elements makes communication more precise and prevents misunderstandings that often arise from text-only descriptions.

One of the most powerful aspects of multimodal AI is its ability to connect different types of information. These systems can read text within images, recognize spatial relationships, detect patterns, and link visual elements to textual concepts.

This ability to integrate visual and textual data opens possibilities for more nuanced and productive interactions. You can ask questions that bridge different types of information, and the AI can provide integrated answers that use its cross-modal strengths.

THE NEXT CHAPTER IN HUMAN-AI INTERACTION

The shift to multimodal AI marks a fundamental change in how we work with machines. Just as we naturally combine speech, gestures, and visuals to share complex ideas, AI is evolving beyond text to understand and communicate through multiple channels.

Think of early computers that could only process numbers, then text, and how limiting that feels compared to today's rich multimedia environment.

We're at a similar turning point with AI. The ability to seamlessly combine images, text, and spatial understanding opens up possibilities that were unimaginable in the text-only era.

But this potential comes with a new challenge: learning to take full advantage of these capabilities. Just as photography and film developed their own languages beyond simply "recorded theater," we need to develop new ways of working with AI that fully use its multimodal nature.

THE FUTURE OF MULTIMODAL PROMPTING

Right now, the multimodal capabilities of AI tools mostly involve text, audio, images, and video. But very soon, there will be new ways to communicate with machines. Ways that feel more natural, more interactive, and more closely aligned with how humans actually think and work.

Multimodal prompting will no longer mean simply uploading a picture or combining text with a diagram. It will become more fluid. You might speak a prompt while gesturing at a screen. You might sketch a wireframe, annotate it with your voice, and have the AI generate code, copy, and layout suggestions based on what you meant, and not just what you said.

It will also become more physical. Wearables, cameras, and sensors could turn body language, tone of voice, and environmental cues into part of the prompt. The way you raise an eyebrow, tap a surface, or pause in your speech may shape how the system responds. Prompts will carry layers of context, emotion, and timing.

This shift will change how we teach, learn, and create. Multimodal prompting will let us approach problems from multiple angles. A legal concept might be explained visually. A data set might be explored through conversation.

The future will belong to those who can think and create in this integrated way. By combining different forms of communication, we can solve problems and design solutions that neither humans nor AI could achieve on their own.

12 Prompting AI Agents

An AI agent is a software program designed to perform tasks or achieve goals independently. It observes its environment, processes information, and takes actions with minimal human input.

However, because AI agents are autonomous, they need carefully crafted prompts. Otherwise, things can go wrong quickly, and you might just end up with an unexpectedly pricey pair of headphones.

Imagine working with an assistant who doesn't just follow orders but thinks ahead, learns from experience, and adapts independently.

This is the promise of AI agents: software systems capable of performing tasks or achieving goals autonomously by understanding their environment, processing information, and **taking action with little or no human intervention.**

UNDERSTANDING AI AGENTS

An AI agent can take on tasks like booking your flights, finding the best restaurants, or even handling your Christmas shopping, provided it has the necessary resources.

What sets AI agents apart from basic programs is their ability to combine three critical capabilities: **perception**, the skill to understand inputs and interpret situations; **reasoning**, the capacity to decide what actions to take based on available information; and **action**, the execution of tasks to achieve their goals.

This blend of abilities allows AI agents to operate with remarkable autonomy, navigating complex tasks in ways that traditional, instruction-based systems cannot.

This ability to work autonomously and adapt in real time makes AI agents highly useful, handling complex tasks that would otherwise require constant human oversight. However, this

autonomy also introduces significant challenges. Autonomous agents can be exploited by malicious actors, posing serious risks to society.

Ensuring the safety and ethical operation of these agents is essential. As they become more independent, strong safeguards, ethical guidelines, and accountability frameworks are needed to prevent misuse and minimize vulnerabilities to cyber-attacks. Without these measures, the risks of autonomous AI could outweigh its potential benefits.

SO, WHAT ACTUALLY IS AN AI AGENT?

Before diving into how to prompt agents effectively, it's important to clarify the term "agent." In AI, the word can mean different things depending on the context. Some people use "agent" to describe workflow systems that follow fixed steps, while others refer to semi-autonomous systems that adapt within set boundaries. At the farthest end of the spectrum, there are fully autonomous agents capable of making independent decisions and dynamically changing their approach.

The term might bring to mind secret agents equipped with gadgets and a tuxedo, but in AI, the real intrigue lies in their adaptability, not their style. When someone mentions an "AI agent," the key question to ask is: What kind of system are we dealing with? Is it more like a structured recipe or a collaborator?

WORKFLOWS TO AGENTS

To better understand agents, it's helpful to contrast them with workflows. **Agentic workflows** are like recipes: a series of fixed steps designed to achieve a specific outcome. These steps are predefined and don't change based on the situation. For example, a customer support workflow might verify a purchase, approve a refund, and send a notification to the customer. Each step is rigid and doesn't adjust if unexpected issues arise.

In contrast, **agents** are like skilled collaborators. They adjust their approach based on circumstances, making decisions and solving problems dynamically. For instance, a customer support agent might retrieve missing information, resolve ambiguous issues, or escalate a tricky case to a human when necessary. This flexibility makes agents powerful but also means they require carefully crafted prompts to guide their actions effectively.

Why is this distinction important? Understanding whether your task is best suited to a workflow or an agent is essential for achieving the best results. Workflows are ideal for predictable tasks where consistency and efficiency are the priority. Agents, however, thrive in dynamic, uncertain environments where adaptability and creative problem-solving are essential.

By recognizing whether your task is more recipe-like (workflow) or requires skilled collaboration (agent), you can design systems and prompts that align with your objectives. This clarity ensures better outcomes and helps you choose the right tool for the job.

BUILDING IN SAFEGUARDS

Effective agent prompting means getting things done responsibly. That requires safeguards that give agents room to act while keeping them aligned with your goals.

Tools like feedback loops, clear boundaries, and decision-making guidelines help maintain the balance between autonomy and accountability. Regular feedback matters. Not to micromanage, but to make timely, useful adjustments that guide behavior in real time.

It also helps to set resource limits, track progress, and prepare for errors with clear protocols.

It might all sound a bit abstract. But give an agent a lazy prompt, and it could spend hours obsessively polishing a landing page or burn through your free credits before you even notice.

FOCUSING ON THE OUTCOME

Prompting agents differs fundamentally from traditional AI interactions. When you chat with a language model, responses come instantly. Type a question, get an answer.

But AI agents operate differently. They work independently over extended periods, gathering information, analyzing data, and synthesizing results. This shift from instant response to prolonged engagement demands a new approach to prompting.

Think of the difference between asking someone for directions and hiring a team of research assistants. With directions, you expect an immediate answer. With a team, you provide objectives, timelines, and expected deliverables. AI agents are more like research assistants than navigation systems.

An agent tasked with producing a research-level report might spend hours scanning databases, evaluating sources, cross-referencing information, and synthesizing findings. During this time, the agent makes countless micro-decisions about relevance, importance, and connection. Each of these decisions stems from the initial prompt.

The stakes are higher with agents than with traditional AI. Imprecise prompts waste resources. Results might miss critical aspects of the intended goal. The cost comes in wasted tokens, unnecessary data processing, lost time, and wrong answers.

> **When prompting an agent, you're not just asking for information. You're initiating a complex process. Your prompt needs to define clear objectives, scope parameters, quality criteria, resource constraints, and output format requirements.**

What stands out is the thought process of agents. It mirrors how a human might approach the task: starting with research, outlining the structure, building the content step by step, and refining for clarity and completeness.

AGENTS NEED CONTEXT TO MAKE GOOD DECISIONS

Imagine your boss gives you an urgent instruction, but all you catch is: "*They asked for it. This is super important and needs to be done today.*" You'd immediately scramble for details. *Who* asked? *What* did they ask for? *Why* is it important? *How* did we handle this last time?

We underestimate just how much implicit information we rely on when making decisions. Context isn't just the immediate request. It's the history behind it, the relationships involved, and the expectations at play.

Human conversations build on a shared history, but LLMs often start fresh with each prompt. Until we provide them with richer context, they won't match the nuance of a trusted colleague.

Without sufficient context, agents risk missing crucial nuances, failing to prioritize correctly, overlooking constraints, or producing outputs that don't align with actual needs.

Constraints, in particular, are not limitations. They are *guiding principles* that help an agent focus its resources effectively. These might include prioritizing specific data sources, emphasizing key aspects of analysis, or adhering to a required format. Well-defined constraints improve efficiency rather than restrict capabilities.

Unlike traditional AI interactions, agents often run for extended periods, creating opportunities for monitoring and adjustment. Good agent prompts should include checkpoints for progress review, criteria for when to seek clarification, parameters for interim updates, and clear stopping conditions.

The difference between a good and great agent prompt often isn't in what it asks for, but in how it guides the process of achieving it. As these systems become more powerful, precise guidance becomes increasingly crucial for effective results.

A LESSON IN AGENTS AND PROMPTING: THE EARPHONES INCIDENT

Consider this real-world example of how even a simple task can go wrong if an agent isn't guided carefully. Recently, I asked an AI agent to find me the cheapest pair of earphones on Amazon. My prompt was straightforward: "Find me the cheapest earphones from Amazon."

The agent diligently went to the website, sorted the results using the "price: low to high" filter, and picked the top option. Or at least, that's what I thought. Instead, the agent accidentally misclicked and sorted the results by "average customer review." Believing the list was sorted by price, it confidently recommended a pair of expensive earphones.

Now imagine if this agent had access to a payment method or resources like a crypto wallet. A seemingly harmless error could have resulted in a costly mistake! This incident highlights the dual challenges of agent autonomy and the importance of precise prompts.

> **What did I do wrong? I failed to provide guardrails. My prompt lacked checks to verify the sorting method or cross-check prices. This illustrates why safeguards, like validating results or setting resource limits, are essential in agent interactions. Autonomous agents can be powerful, but they also require careful oversight to prevent errors.**

LOOKING FORWARD

Think about it: you are giving instructions to an independent system capable of making its own decisions. This is both an incredible opportunity and a profound responsibility. Effective prompting requires thoughtful balance and providing clear guidance while granting agents the autonomy to adapt.

This balance is dynamic and will shift as agents become more capable. Yet the fundamental principles of effective prompting remain the same: clarity, context, and intent.

Agents, by their nature, are autonomous. This autonomy can lead to powerful outcomes, but it also means they must be guided with extraordinary care. Prompts are not just instructions; they are the scaffolding of the agent's behavior.

Every word you choose has the potential to shape how the system interprets and acts on its environment. Crafting them well ensures the agent aligns with human values and intentions while avoiding the risks of unrestrained autonomy.

What we craft now in prompts and safeguards sets the foundation for the responsible use of increasingly powerful AI. Approaching this task with care ensures that agents remain tools for human benefit, fostering innovation while mitigating risks.

13 Prompting is a Moral Act

In AI, ethics often feels like PR, a polished surface hiding deeper problems. Companies talk about fairness and transparency, but their efforts rarely go beyond vague promises. These conversations are more about image than accountability.

But it doesn't have to be this way.

This chapter was difficult to write. Not because the techniques are complex, but because I wanted to say more. Much more. There is a vast and urgent conversation to be had about AI ethics. But that is not the purpose of this chapter.

The point here is simpler, though no less important: **prompting is a moral act.** It is not just a technical input or a productivity hack. Every prompt shapes how AI systems interpret the world and interact with it.

When we write a prompt, we do more than instruct. We influence how AI presents information, makes suggestions, and frames decisions. These outputs can scale quickly and touch many lives. The stakes are not hypothetical.

This chapter will not attempt a deep dive into AI ethics. That deserves its own book—several, in fact. What we will do is acknowledge something essential: **prompting carries moral weight, and we can begin making more thoughtful, more ethical choices right now.**

PROMPTING AS A MORAL ACT

The gap between ethical principles and practice exists in every industry. In AI, this gap is especially significant. Prompting is an active process that embeds values, priorities, and assumptions into AI-generated outputs. These choices shape interactions, influence user behavior, and reinforce certain perspectives.

This chapter does not provide a checklist for "ethical prompting." Ethical decisions require context, awareness, and the ability to anticipate impact. A prompt is not just a technical instruction but a factor in shaping AI's role in the world.

AI ethics frameworks rely on broad principles, assuming that defining fairness and transparency will lead to responsible outcomes. In practice, this approach often fails.

Ethical guidelines frequently exist without enforcement. Companies can claim a commitment to fairness and transparency, but without ways to track or measure adherence, these claims remain unverified. Transparency without verification does not create accountability.

Many frameworks also encourage checklist thinking, reducing complex ethical questions to a series of rules. This can create the appearance of compliance while ignoring deeper issues. Ethical prompting, like ethical AI design, requires awareness of context and long-term consequences.

Timing is another major weakness. Ethics often enters the conversation after key technical milestones have shaped an AI system's behavior. Late-stage adjustments become difficult or impossible. Responsible AI requires early attention to ethics, not last-minute fixes.

Furthermore, ethical values vary across cultures. Prompting needs to account for these differences while maintaining core principles. What constitutes fairness, respect, or appropriate content can differ significantly across societies and communities. A prompt that seems neutral to its creator might embed cultural assumptions that privilege certain perspectives over others.

BUILDING BETTER SYSTEMS

Ethical AI development requires more than advisory boards and aspirational statements. It needs systems that make ethical considerations a core part of design, rather than an afterthought.

Companies that take this seriously create processes where

ethics is considered alongside functionality, not separate from it. This means involving ethics experts in development decisions, giving them real authority rather than advisory roles that can be ignored.

Professional standards must also evolve. AI development is often seen as a purely technical discipline, but ethical reasoning should be part of every practitioner's skill set. Those designing and deploying AI need both technical expertise and the ability to assess the broader implications of their work.

In high-risk applications, human oversight is essential. AI functions best when combined with human judgment, not when left to operate without constraints. Ensuring that systems are reviewed, challenged, and refined by human decision-makers reduces the risks of automation bias and unchecked algorithmic influence.

PROMPTING FOR ENVIRONMENTAL AND SOCIAL JUSTICE

AI systems depend on real-world resources. Every AI query consumes electricity, water, and processing power. Large-scale AI models require significant infrastructure, and data centers supporting these systems contribute to increasing energy demands.

A single prompt may seem insignificant, but when multiplied across millions of interactions, inefficient prompting has measurable consequences. Poorly optimized prompts can increase processing time, drive up infrastructure costs, and expand AI's environmental footprint.

AI models do not just generate words or pictures. They also consume energy with every response.

Reducing unnecessary computation benefits both organizations and the environment. A well-structured prompt minimizes redundant processing while maintaining accuracy. An efficient system does not waste time or resources, allowing AI to perform at its best without excessive consumption.

Organizations that optimize AI interactions improve both their financial bottom line and their sustainability efforts.

BUILDING RESPONSIBLE SYSTEMS

Prompting decisions influences both system performance and ethical impact. Ethical prompting requires awareness of how AI processes information, allocates resources, and affects users. Every interaction shapes future interactions.

Once a flawed prompt has been widely used, its effects might become embedded in the AI's outputs, influencing responses in ways that are difficult to reverse.

> **A responsible approach to prompting involves setting clear expectations for accuracy, fairness, and efficiency. A well-crafted prompt reduces bias, directs AI toward useful insights, and avoids unnecessary computational strain.**

Ethical prompting is not just about avoiding harm; it is about ensuring that AI systems operate effectively, fairly, and sustainably. The difference between a careless prompt and a well-considered one can be the difference between an AI system that misinforms and one that helps people make better decisions.

DRAWING ON MORAL PHILOSOPHY

Understanding the ethics of prompting requires looking beyond technical concerns to the values that shape human decision-making. Philosophy provides a foundation for thinking through ethical dilemmas, especially in cases where simple solutions do not exist.

Collective ethics is particularly relevant. A single prompt may not seem like it has much impact, but in aggregate, prompts guide the evolution of AI systems. The way AI is prompted today determines how it will function in the future. Recognizing this cumulative effect makes ethical prompting an ongoing responsibility rather than a one-time decision.

BUILDING AN ETHICAL FUTURE

Ethical prompting cannot be an afterthought. As AI systems become more powerful, ethical concerns will only grow more urgent. Those who engage with AI now set the standards for how it will be used in the future.

Many organizations struggle with AI ethics because there are no universal standards, no enforcement, and no consistent consequences for failing to meet ethical goals. At the same time, commercial pressures push ethical concerns aside.

> **AI users can take immediate steps to improve outcomes. Questioning assumptions, prompting for multiple perspectives, and testing for bias can improve results in real time.**

For now, it is important to recognize that prompts are not meaningless. They carry weight. They consume energy. And they have the potential to shape the future, one interaction at a time.

14 Vibe Everything

First came Vibe Coding. You told the AI how something should feel, not how it should work. Now, it's Vibe Everything.

In February 2025, Andrej Karpathy, a renowned AI researcher and former OpenAI co-founder, shared a peculiar observation on his X account:

> **There's a new kind of coding I call "vibe coding," where you fully give in to the vibes, embrace exponentials, and forget that the code even exists. It's possible because the LLMs (e.g., Cursor Composer w Sonnet) are getting too good. Also I just talk to Composer with SuperWhisper, so I barely even touch the keyboard. I ask for the dumbest things, like "decrease the padding on the sidebar by half," because I'm too lazy to find it. I "Accept All" always; I don't read the diffs anymore. When I get error messages, I just copy and paste them in with no comment; usually that fixes it. The code grows beyond my usual comprehension; I'd have to really read through it for a while. Sometimes the LLMs can't fix a bug, so I just work around it or ask for random changes until it goes away. It's not too bad for throwaway weekend projects, but still quite amusing. I'm building a project or webapp, but it's not really coding—I just see stuff, say stuff, run stuff, and copy paste stuff, and it mostly works.**

What begins as a tongue-in-cheek confession reveals something deeper: **a fundamental shift in how humans interact with technology.**

THE DAWN OF VIBE CODING

Vibe coding represents a new relationship with programming.

> **Instead of writing precise lines of code, developers now use natural language prompts rich in tone, reference, and mood to guide AI systems toward desired outcomes.**
>
> **The programmer no longer writes in a formal syntax but speaks in *feelings* and *intentions*. You say what something should *feel like*, not exactly how it should work.**

This shift does more than simplify tasks. It *reconfigures* the nature of creativity and execution. The programmer becomes less an architect and more a conductor, shaping direction through suggestion and rhythm rather than control and specification. AI fills in the rest, often in ways the human may not fully understand until later, if ever.

THE HISTORICAL ARC

This transformation is the latest step in how we relate to computers. In the beginning, we had to speak their language—using punch cards and command lines. Then came graphical interfaces, which introduced familiar metaphors like desktops and folders. Touchscreens followed, letting us interact through gestures and taps. Voice assistants brought another shift, allowing us to speak and be understood in simple ways. Each of these moments moved us closer to a more natural way of interacting with machines.

But these were all incremental steps. *Vibing* represents something more profound: computers finally adapting to our natural mode of thinking rather than forcing us to adapt to theirs. The historical pendulum seems to be swinging from humans accommodating machine logic to machines accommodating *human intuition*.

BEYOND CODE

This new approach is not limited to code. As AI tools become more advanced and easier to access, the same style of interaction is beginning to appear in other professional domains. The vibe is spreading.

In **law**, practitioners are beginning to "vibe" with AI to draft contracts, write briefs, and interpret case law. Rather than start from scratch or follow rigid templates, a lawyer might prompt an assistant with, "*Give me something like the previous settlement but tougher on IP and with a friendlier tone.*" The AI responds with language that reflects not only the legal structure but also the strategic mood behind the request. It becomes a conversation about intent, not just compliance.

In **medicine**, doctors are experimenting with diagnostic systems that respond not only to data but also to the tone of clinical intuition. A physician might say, "*This reminds me of a case from last month. The vitals are similar, but this one feels more urgent.*" These kinds of inputs, vague as they may be, allow the AI to combine pattern recognition with contextual inference, producing responses that feel more like collaboration than computation.

Designers have been among the earliest adopters of this sensibility. A prompt might sound like, "*I want something that feels midcentury but digital, something asymmetric and in motion.*" From this kind of instruction, AI can generate dozens of variations, refining based on feedback that is equally intuitive.

> **This is the idea of Vibe Everything. The prompter does not describe the output. They describe the *vibe* of the output. And the system responds accordingly.**

SOCIETAL TRANSFORMATIONS

This shift carries profound implications for our institutions. Educational systems, which have traditionally focused on teaching formal languages and structured thinking, now face a dilemma. Do they continue teaching coding syntax when natural language prompting might become the dominant interface?

Some forward-thinking schools are already developing "vibe coding" courses alongside traditional programming, recognizing that mastery of *nuance* and *suggestion* may become as valuable as algorithmic thinking.

Professional development is also transforming. Companies increasingly value what might be called collaborative intuition: the ability to guide AI systems toward desired outcomes without prescriptive instructions.

This skill transcends technical domains, creating new career paths for those who can effectively *speak vibe* across disciplines. Organizations are beginning to restructure around these capabilities, with flatter hierarchies built around AI-human partnerships rather than traditional chains of command.

THE MECHANICS BEHIND THE MAGIC

So why does "vibe" work? The answer lies in the structure of large language models themselves. These models operate in a massive latent space, a multidimensional conceptual map built on billions of data points.

> **When you use a prompt filled with tone, reference, or stylistic intent, you are activating particular regions of that space. You are pointing, softly, and the model fills in the direction with plausible detail.**

Modern AI systems are not just good at literal reasoning. They are remarkably adept at handling ambiguity, inference, and incomplete information. They do not simply follow instructions. They *infer* what you mean, how you feel, and what kind of response might fit the situation.

There is also a deep psychological alignment at play. Vibing feels natural to humans because it mimics how we already communicate. Most people do not think in formulas or frameworks. They think in stories, in impressions and in references that make sense to them but may not translate cleanly into a specification. Traditional systems forced us to formalize these instincts. Vibing lets us work more directly with them.

THE SHADOW SIDE

Of course, this freedom comes with risk. As Karpathy notes, when you vibe too far, you may no longer understand what the system is doing. The code becomes something you accept blindly. You hope for the best.

And sometimes, that is fine, especially for small experiments or side projects. But for systems that demand reliability or explainability, this creates a dangerous distance between intent and outcome.

The trust dynamic grows more complicated. How do we remain appropriately skeptical while still embracing these powerful tools? Would you trust a vibe-driven lawyer with a bet-the-company lawsuit? Or a vibe-based diagnosis from your doctor? Is that vibe-coded app truly ready for production—especially when security is on the line?

Part of the craft is knowing when to vibe and when to dig deep.

There are also questions of dependency and long-term skill erosion. If professionals rely too heavily on vibe-based prompting, they may lose touch with the principles behind the output. The creative process becomes reactive rather than generative.

THE NEW FRONTIER

Yet for all its limitations, the vibe shift is already underway. You can see it in how people use AI tools today. They stop explaining and start gesturing. They improvise, adjust, sense the tone, and try again. The creative loop becomes looser, faster, and more intuitive. And for many, more fun.

What makes the vibe approach feel so different is that it dissolves the hard edges between thinking and doing. The interface disappears. The mental translation fades. You are no longer programming, writing, designing, or diagnosing in a formal way. You are simply *thinking out loud,* and something on the other side is listening well enough to keep up.

"Vibe" is a buzzword, and in a few years (or even a few months) it will probably sound dated, even nostalgic. "Remember the vibe coding epidemic in 2025?"

But the idea behind it is not going anywhere. The shift toward intuition, iteration, and less explicit reasoning is already changing how we work and create. It is the beginning of a different kind of cognitive partnership. A new way of making things real. And we are only just starting to understand what it might become.

15 Beyond Human-Level

The real revolution in AI isn't about matching human-level performance. It's about creating new forms of intelligence that enhance and expand what we can do.

We're too focused on copying human abilities when we could aim much higher. AI doesn't need to follow human structures or settle for being an "assistant." It can help us think, work, and create in ways we've never imagined.

When early scientists tried to understand how birds fly, they focused on mimicking wing-flapping. Initial attempts at human flight involved mechanical wings that flapped, imitating birds. These efforts, however, failed spectacularly.

Real progress only came when researchers **stopped copying nature** and began studying the principles of lift and aerodynamics. This shift led to fixed-wing flight, a breakthrough that allows planes to soar higher and faster than any bird.

Today, we face a similar turning point with artificial intelligence. The urge to make AI think and act like humans not only limits its potential but also misunderstands what intelligence can be.

This chapter focuses not on making AI more human-like or chasing "human-level" benchmarks, but on moving past those constraints to explore new forms of intelligence and capability.

THE HUMAN BENCHMARK PROBLEM

Much of our thinking about AI is stuck on imitation. We fixate on making it behave like us, think like us and sound like us. This goes beyond simple anthropomorphism. It shapes how we design, measure, and evaluate these systems. We cheer when AI writes like a journalist, plays like a grandmaster, or diagnoses like a doctor.

But this is like judging a submarine by how well it swims.

By holding AI to human standards, we risk missing its potential to solve problems in ways we never could.

Consider the breakthrough in protein folding. For years, researchers tried to teach machines to think like biochemists. Progress was slow. Then DeepMind's AlphaFold took a different route. It didn't replicate human reasoning. It developed its own strategies and outperformed every expert in the field.

This isn't a one-off. Across many disciplines, real breakthroughs happen when we stop asking AI to mimic us and start allowing it to invent its own paths. The challenge is not to make AI more human but to imagine what intelligence could be when it's not shaped by our reflection.

CENTAUR CHESS AND THE FUTURE OF HUMAN-AI COLLABORATION

The story of chess and AI reveals important lessons about how humans and AI can work together.

In the early days, chess computers were weak, barely able to beat amateur players. But as they improved, something remarkable happened: the strongest players weren't humans or computers alone, but teams called "**centaurs.**" In these teams, humans focused on strategy while computers handled calculations.

This seemed like the perfect solution, a blueprint for how humans and AI could collaborate in the future. But it didn't work out that way.

The centaur phase, once seen as the future of chess, turned out to be surprisingly brief. Today, no human can compete with the top chess engines like Stockfish. Even my old MacBook with a broken fan can easily defeat the world champion, Magnus Carlsen.

AI has advanced even further with programs like AlphaGo, which surpassed human knowledge entirely by learning through self-play, without relying on human input. The human part of the centaur had become a liability rather than an asset.

Yet chess didn't die. In fact, it exploded in popularity!

More people play chess today than ever before. Chess players stopped trying to compete with AI entirely. Instead, they use chess engines as powerful tools for learning and discovery. Young players improve faster than ever before, while grandmasters explore new strategies they never would have discovered on their own. They're not trying to beat the machines anymore. They're using them to push the boundaries of human creativity and understanding.

The lesson is clear. Framing humans as the ones who just "fix AI's mistakes" leads nowhere. Instead of resisting what AI can do, we should rethink how we contribute. Just as chess players adapted to superhuman AI, professionals in every field need to find new ways to create value in an AI-driven world.

The surprise in chess wasn't just that AI became unbeatable. It was that it didn't matter so much.

The centaur era of chess was a stepping stone to something bigger, but not in the way anyone predicted. The same could be true for many fields today. Human-AI collaboration isn't about competition; it's about evolving together to shape the future of work. Sometimes that means letting go of our assumptions about how humans and AI should work together and being open to completely new possibilities.

And like chess, the most surprising outcome may be that surpassing human abilities doesn't necessarily reduce human involvement. It simply transforms it in unexpected ways.

THE COMFORT OF FAMILIAR METAPHORS

Why do we gravitate toward human metaphors for AI? The answer lies in how we adapt to new technologies.

When graphical user interfaces were first introduced, designers used *skeuomorphic elements.*

Skeuomorphic means designing new technology to mimic the appearance of familiar physical objects.

Notepads looked like yellow legal paper, complete with lines and margins; calendars mimicked the look of leather-bound books; even the "trash" icon was designed as a physical wastepaper basket.

These metaphors helped users transition to digital tools, but they also limited what was possible. Only when designers moved beyond these physical-world constraints did they discover the true potential of digital interfaces.

Similarly, we cling to human-like metaphors for AI because they're familiar. We ask it to "think like" various professionals because these roles are understandable. But just as skeuomorphic design limited early digital interfaces, human metaphors constrain what AI can achieve.

FROM SKEUOMORPHISM TO PROFESSIONAL CONSTRAINTS

This pattern of limiting innovation through familiar metaphors extends beyond interface design into how entire professions approach AI. Just as early digital designers felt compelled to replicate physical objects, professionals today unconsciously recreate their organizational structures and workflows in AI systems.

This phenomenon is captured by *Conway's Law,* a principle originally observed in software development:

"Organizations which design systems are constrained to produce designs which are copies of the communication structures of these organizations."

Consider how this plays out across different professions:

In **law**, firms design AI systems that mirror their rigid pyramid structures and hierarchical workflows. The AI becomes a "junior associate," assigned basic tasks while partners handle "strategic work." This recreates the same pecking order that constrains human lawyers. While this makes AI comprehensible to legal professionals, it prevents us from reimagining legal services beyond traditional firm structures.

In **healthcare**, doctors design AI systems that mirror hospital hierarchies and specialist workflows. The AI becomes a "digital resident," following the same chain of command and consultation patterns. This familiar structure might prevent us from discovering entirely new approaches to patient care.

In **education**, we see AI tools designed as "digital teaching assistants," reinforcing traditional classroom dynamics. The AI takes attendance, grades assignments, and provides tutoring.

These are all useful tasks, but all rooted in centuries-old models of learning. What might become possible if we reimagined education without these inherited structures?

THE PROFESSIONAL IDENTITY TRAP

These aren't just simple analogies. They represent deep-seated professional identities and organizational structures that shape how we think about AI's potential. Each profession brings its own mental models, hierarchies, and workflow patterns to AI development.

The very expertise that makes professionals valuable in their field can create blind spots when imagining AI's potential. A surgeon might envision AI as a more precise version of themselves while missing opportunities for AI to transform pre-operative planning or post-operative care in ways that don't fit traditional surgical workflows.

> **Just as digital design eventually broke free from skeuomorphic constraints—giving us interfaces that leverage the unique properties of digital spaces—we need to break free from professional skeuomorphism in AI development.**

This requires several key shifts:

1. **Cross-Pollination of Ideas:** When healthcare professionals work with artists, when lawyers collaborate with social workers, when educators partner with game designers—new possibilities emerge. These unexpected collaborations help break down professional constraints and reveal new approaches.
2. **Questioning Fundamental Structures:** Every profession needs to examine its basic assumptions: Why do we organize work this way? What would our services look like if we started from scratch today? How might AI capabilities suggest entirely new organizational structures?
3. **Embracing Diversity in Design:** Different backgrounds bring different mental models. A diverse design team is more likely to question embedded assumptions and imagine novel approaches. This diversity should extend beyond professional background to include cultural, socioeconomic, and cognitive diversity.

BEYOND ROLE-PLAYING PROMPTS

One clear example of Conway's Law in action is our habit of role-based prompting, like asking AI to "act like" specific human professionals.

When lawyers ask AI to "think like a junior associate" or doctors request it to "act as a medical resident," they're unconsciously recreating their organizational hierarchies in AI interactions.

> **While role-based prompts can be useful starting points, they fundamentally restrict AI's potential when applied too rigidly.**

Instead of casting AI in pre-set professional roles, we should explore how it might transcend traditional organizational structures entirely.

Rather than asking it to "*think like a junior lawyer*" (and thus constraining it to tasks we consider appropriate for that role), we can prompt it to approach legal problems from entirely new angles that aren't bound by traditional firm hierarchies.

Better prompts begin with recognizing how our professional structures unconsciously shape our expectations of AI. When we ask AI to "*write like a partner*" or "*analyze like an associate,*" we impose our organizational constraints on a technology that could potentially transform these very structures.

Prompts often reveal how we think about AI. When we ask it to "*analyze data like a scientist*," we impose limits. These prompts reflect our tendency to view AI as an extension of ourselves, a tool to mimic human intelligence rather than to expand beyond it.

But what if, instead, we used prompts to tap into the qualities that make AI unique?

ABUNDANT INTELLIGENCE

Moving beyond human metaphors requires us to rethink what we mean by intelligence. Biological limits bind human intelligence. We think sequentially, can only focus on a few things at a time, and our cognitive abilities are limited by our brains. AI, however, doesn't face these constraints.

AI can process multiple perspectives simultaneously, explore entire solution spaces in one go, connect across massive datasets, and generate countless possibilities in parallel.

This isn't just "faster" thinking; it's fundamentally *different* thinking. Yet, we rarely tap into these unique capabilities because we keep asking AI to work within human constraints. By letting go of these limits, we can explore a world of abundant *intelligence,* where intelligence is not scarce or linear but available in vast, varied forms.

To break free from traditional approaches to AI, we need to change how we engage with it. Rather than looking for a single "correct" answer, we can use AI to explore multiple possibilities simultaneously.

Instead of a sequential analysis, we can leverage AI's ability to map out entire possibility spaces, simultaneously examining multiple dimensions of a problem.

Consider a design challenge. Instead of asking AI to create one solution, we could prompt it to map the landscape of potential solutions, explore divergent approaches, identify patterns across options, and even propose hybrids by combining different elements. Give me 10 suggestions!

Humans have a deeply ingrained sense of not wanting to bother others, a trait rooted in social norms and empathy. But when it comes to AI, this instinct becomes a limitation. Unlike humans, AI doesn't tire, get annoyed, or judge.

You can "bother" AI endlessly. Ask it a thousand questions, refine the same prompt over and over, or explore ideas without hesitation.

This freedom to experiment, iterate, and learn without fear of judgment is a true game-changer.

THE NEW HUMAN ROLE: CURATOR OF INTELLIGENCE

As we move beyond human metaphors for AI, our roles also change. Instead of competing with AI, we become *curators of abundance,* responsible for managing and making sense of AI's extensive outputs. This role requires new skills in intelligence curation, pattern recognition, and strategic direction.

- *Intelligence curation* involves selecting and combining insights from AI's diverse outputs, making sense of the array of solutions.
- *Pattern recognition* allows us to identify meaningful connections across AI-generated perspectives, uncovering trends and themes that might otherwise be invisible.
- *Strategic direction* enables us to guide AI exploration, steering its vast capacity toward valuable insights while staying open to unexpected discoveries.

This shift doesn't make human intelligence obsolete; rather, it allows us to work with new forms of intelligence in more sophisticated ways.

A PRACTICAL GUIDE TO BREAKING FREE

Moving beyond human-centered metaphors requires deliberate practice and a shift in mindset. The first step is recognizing when we're imposing unnecessary human constraints on AI. When we automatically ask it to "write like a human" or "think like an expert" without considering alternative approaches.

Next, reframe your questions. Instead of asking, "*How would a human do this?*" Try, "*What's the best way to approach this problem with AI's capabilities in mind?*" This shift encourages you to seek solutions that leverage AI's unique strengths, rather than limiting it to human modes of thinking.

Finally, integrate AI into workflows that blend both human and AI capabilities. For example, let AI explore vast solution spaces while you focus on refining and selecting the most relevant insights. This collaboration combines the creative problem-solving strengths of both human and artificial intelligence.

A NEW HORIZON FOR AI COLLABORATION

The future of AI isn't about making machines more human-like; it's about discovering entirely new ways of thinking and working together. Moving beyond human-centered metaphors allows us to envision intelligence in new forms, evolving our collaboration with AI in unprecedented ways.

This shift requires us to release anthropomorphic constraints and embrace new paradigms. By reimagining intelligence and problem-solving, we can tap into AI's ability to work on a scale and scope far beyond our own.

We are at a turning point in human-AI collaboration. Like early aviation pioneers who moved beyond wing-flapping to achieve powered flight, we need to let go of the idea of "human-like" intelligence to unlock AI's full potential. This is more than just a technical shift. It represents a fundamental change in how we understand and utilize intelligence.

The true revolution in AI isn't about achieving human-level performance; it's about exploring new forms of intelligence that complement and elevate human abilities.

This is the next frontier, a space where human and artificial intelligence come together to create solutions, insights, and innovations that neither could accomplish alone.

BEYOND TRAFFIC LIGHTS AND SIDEWALKS: HUMAN VALUE IN AN AI WORLD

One common mistake is measuring human value by our ability to outperform AI. When we obsess over AI's limitations or deny its superhuman capabilities, we trap ourselves in a defensive position, trying to protect the status quo instead of growing alongside these powerful tools.

Human value doesn't lie in solving CAPTCHAs or counting sidewalks in blurry photos. Being able to spot a motorbike in an image isn't what makes you human.

This isn't about ignoring AI's risks. Those need serious attention and management. However, defining human worth solely by what AI can't do underestimates us.

We're more than the tasks machines struggle with. Clinging to areas where we still outperform AI is a losing strategy as these technologies continue to advance.

By accepting AI's superhuman abilities, we can focus on a more exciting question: how do we want to evolve as humans in this new era? This shift in thinking doesn't diminish humanity. It expands it. Working with AI rather than against it opens up new possibilities for human achievement and meaning. **The goal isn't to stay *ahead* of AI but to use it as a springboard for human growth and discovery.**

16 The Death of Prompt Engineering

There's a skill set beyond the basics of "prompt engineering" that will always matter, even as AI gets better at understanding us.

These are timeless skills: the curiosity to explore, the courage to experiment, the patience to refine, and the ability to express ideas clearly.

For a while, prompt engineering felt like digital magic. Carefully choosing the right words could transform a clunky AI assistant into something brilliant. Communities quietly shared "magic phrases," each one feeling like the secret to tapping into AI's full potential.

But now? The magic is fading. Or at least, it's evolving. Prompt engineering, as we know it, is changing. Not because it's becoming completely irrelevant but because both AI and its users are growing up.

And to be honest, I never liked the "*engineer*" part. Engineering is something entirely different. Let's not mix them up.

Prompting today is about communication. It's expressive, interpretive, even playful. Calling it engineering kind of misses the point. It ignores the creative, conversational way we work with these models.

And let's be real: someone who spent six years studying thermodynamics might cringe at the idea that asking for a cat-themed haiku counts as *engineering*.

FROM GUESSWORK TO SELF-OPTIMIZATION

Remember when crafting a great prompt felt like a guessing game?

Should you phrase it as a command? Add polite language? Throw in an elaborate backstory for no reason? Maybe sprinkle in some urgency: "The ship is sinking, and you need to answer quickly, or people will die!"

Half the time, success felt like sheer luck.

Now, AI systems are taking the guesswork out of the process. Modern tools can *optimize their own inputs* to get better results. Ask something as simple as, "*Help me plan a marketing strategy*," and instead of stumbling, the AI can refine your vague request into something actionable.

Researchers have even tested this. In one experiment, AI was tasked with solving fundamental math problems using two types of prompts: ones crafted by humans and ones generated by the AI itself. The AI-designed prompts outperformed their human-made counterparts, and some were downright strange.

Case in point: one of the **best-performing prompts** wasn't a question or a statement but a full-blown Star Trek scenario:

> "Command, we need you to plot a course through this turbulence and locate the source of the anomaly. Use all available data and your expertise to guide us through this challenging situation."

This gave the best results! But why?

Because AI doesn't process language the way we do. It works mathematically, juggling probabilities and connections. Dramatic, unexpected phrasing can trigger responses we'd never predict.

Spending hours agonizing over the perfect prompt phrasing might soon be a thing of the past. AI is learning to do that for us, and sometimes it comes up with approaches we would not have even considered.

BETTER TOOLS, FEWER TRICKS

It's not just the AI itself that's improving. The interfaces we use to interact with these systems are getting smarter.

Have you noticed how new tools let you adjust sliders, select roles, or toggle creativity levels? Want a formal report? Click the "Analyst" button. Craving a bit of whimsy? Dial up the creativity. Want "Deep Thinking"? Click here.

This evolution suggests that the era of crafting prompts like an artisan is winding down. Instead, we're moving toward a world where users focus on *what* they want while the tools handle the *how*.

Modern models are far better at understanding natural language. They're attuned to intent. You no longer need to tinker endlessly with your prompt to get a coherent response.

And soon, even that tinkering will disappear.

THINKING TOOLS NEED LESS HAND-HOLDING

The new generation of AI tools is starting to think more like, well, *thinking partners*.

Remember when we had to meticulously break everything down for models? Getting quality responses meant spelling things out step by step, adding explicit logic, and creating structured frameworks.

That era is ending. Today's models better grasp our intentions. With reasoning capabilities built in, you can present a rough, incomplete thought, and they'll typically find an intelligent way to respond. No excessive explanation is needed.

Surprisingly, too much structure can actually hinder performance. Natural, conversational language often works better than rigidly structured prompts with forced reasoning patterns.

This marks a subtle but significant shift: from programming to *conversation*, from control to collaboration.

As these tools become more adept at thinking independently, our role simplifies. Ask thoughtful questions. Communicate clearly. Then step back and let them work.

THE RISE OF CONTEXT ENGINEERING

While everyone's busy announcing the death of prompt engineering, something more interesting is happening behind the scenes. We're not prompting less. We're just getting much better at the infrastructure around it.

In the early days, we obsessed over how to phrase things. Everyone had their favorite tricks. Starting with "*you are an expert in...*" or saying "*think step by step*" gave your prompt a little extra magic.

But these days, that's often not enough. The systems are becoming more dynamic, and single prompts rarely cut it. This is especially true with agents performing complex tasks.

> What really matters is delivering the right information to the model, at the right time, in the right format. That's context engineering.

The term is gaining traction because it captures something essential about modern agentic systems: the systematic delivery of relevant information.

In the agents section of this book, we explored how human interactions naturally build on shared history and context. AI agents, by contrast, start every interaction with a blank slate. This is why giving them the right amount of context is crucial for good decision-making. It's also why they often need tools to search for additional context when necessary.

Context engineering can involve giving an agent access to tools that help it gather information. It might involve building memory so the AI can recall past interactions. Whatever the method, the goal is the same: to provide context that is accurate, timely, and useful.

This is still prompting, just at a higher level. We are no longer crafting one-off inputs. We are building systems that adapt to changing data and know how to shape it appropriately every time.

Of course, there is still an optimization puzzle at the heart of it. What counts as enough context? Too little, and the model flies blind. Too much, and you either hit token limits or lose clarity in the noise.

Context is still king. One of the most common reasons agentic systems underperform is not a lack of intelligence or power. It is a lack of the right context.

"IT'S JUST RESTING"

So, is prompt engineering dead? To borrow a line from Monty Python: *"It's not dead; it's just resting!"*

Sure, the process is becoming less hands-on, but that doesn't mean it's irrelevant. The principles behind good prompting—clarity, context, and intent—will remain critical.

You'll still need to guide the system, evaluate its outputs, and shape its direction. The role of the "prompt engineer" is evolving into that of a collaborator, working alongside AI rather than simply programming it.

And let's not forget: the weird, creative, and surprising aspects of prompting aren't going anywhere. After all, who could have guessed that pretending to be Captain Kirk would make an AI better at math?

These moments of uncertainty remind us that while AI is becoming more innovative, it's still full of surprises. For those who enjoy the experimental, almost playful side of prompting, there will always be room to push boundaries and uncover something unexpected.

Prompt engineering is growing up. The days of magic spells might be winding down, but what's emerging is even more exciting: a partnership between humans and AI that's more intuitive, more collaborative, and still just as capable of surprising us.

So yeah, it's kind of dead.

But no need to mourn the "death" of prompt engineering. Let's throw it a party instead. Because what's coming next is stranger, weirder, and more delightful. And way more powerful.

Part 2

Practical Techniques and Applications

17 Finding Your Voice

There's no one right way to work with AI. Some people craft detailed, structured prompts, while others prefer a more casual conversation. Some lean on technical terms, while others stick to simple, everyday language.

The best approach is the one that feels natural to you. Find your own voice.

One of the most exciting discoveries about AI is that everyone has their own unique way of interacting with it. Over time, people develop a style that mirrors their thought process, and this style can become one of their greatest strengths. Rather than following a universal right way of prompting, effective users find what works best for *them,* adapting the technology to their natural way of thinking.

Working with AI isn't about rigidly following "best practices." Instead, it's like building a relationship with a highly intelligent (though sometimes unpredictable) collaborator.

Success with AI doesn't depend on simply following rules but on finding a voice that feels *authentic* to you. Like any creative partnership, the relationship you develop with AI takes time, experimentation, and perhaps even a few missteps along the way.

This book shows various prompting approaches, but don't feel constrained by them. Use them as starting points, adapt what works, and discard what doesn't.

Your unique background and way of thinking might lead you to approaches we haven't even considered. That's not just okay—it's exactly how this field will evolve."

THE POWER OF PERSONAL PROMPTING STYLES

Interestingly, the way people approach prompting often reflects how they think, learn, and solve problems in other areas of life. This personal style is a key asset and can take different forms.

Over time, I've observed three primary prompting styles that seem to work well across a variety of users: the **Architect, the Explorer, and the Conductor. Let's explore each in more depth.**

The Architect: Building a Strong Foundation

Architects are methodical, systematic thinkers.

They approach AI with a clear plan, breaking down complex requests into smaller, manageable steps. Their prompts often look like technical specifications or carefully structured project briefs, guiding the AI toward a specific goal. Architects tend to excel at tasks that require precision and clarity. Whether they're designing a new AI process or conducting a detailed analysis, their structured approach keeps the AI on track.

> ***Example*: Think of an Architect as someone drafting the blueprint for a building. Every detail is carefully specified, each step meticulously planned, resulting in a solid, reliable structure. For Architect-style prompters, clarity is everything. They start by defining their exact objective, lay out each part of the prompt, and build toward the final output step-by-step.**

The Explorer: Embracing the Process

Explorers, by contrast, dive into AI as if on an adventure.

They begin with open-ended questions, follow unexpected paths, and let curiosity guide them. Their prompts feel like conversations—looser, less structured, but rich with possibilities. While this approach can feel unpredictable, it often leads to surprising insights and creative breakthroughs. Explorers might not always know exactly where they're headed, but they excel at spotting opportunities as they emerge.

> ***Example*: Picture a traveler setting off with no fixed destination, open to discovering whatever lies ahead. In the AI realm, an Explorer might start with a broad question—"How could we rethink this design?"—and let the AI's responses inspire new directions. This style may appear unstructured, but it can lead to insights and ideas that a more rigid approach might overlook.**

The Conductor: Orchestrating Complexity

Conductors are the people who can manage multiple threads simultaneously, weaving together different aspects of a problem into a cohesive solution.

They use AI to run parallel conversations: one thread might focus on technical details, another on creative options, and a third on potential challenges. By synthesizing these threads, Conductors arrive at solutions that are both comprehensive and nuanced.

> ***Example*: Think of an orchestra conductor guiding various instruments to create a harmonious piece. The Conductor in AI interaction does something similar, balancing multiple angles to achieve a holistic view. This style is especially effective for complex projects requiring multidimensional thinking, such as project management or strategic planning.**

Of course, these are just rough stereotypes. But it can be useful and even fun to think about which one is closest to your own style. All of them can work well.

FINDING YOUR STYLE—AND LETTING IT EVOLVE

Most people begin their AI journey by following standard prompting templates. You'll often see these in guides and tutorials as "best practices" for prompting. While these templates are helpful, they're just the starting point.

As you grow more comfortable, you'll likely develop a more intuitive style that matches your own way of thinking. This transition—from following set instructions to finding your unique voice—is what makes working with AI truly personal and powerful.

Think of it like learning a new language. At first, you rely on textbook phrases, carefully constructed sentences, and grammar rules. But true fluency comes when you start thinking *in* that language.

In AI, prompting fluency arrives when you find ways to express yourself naturally, adapting to each task while staying true to your authentic style.

PRACTICAL TIPS FOR DEVELOPING YOUR PROMPTING VOICE

- **Experiment:** Try out different prompting methods, from highly structured to open-ended, to discover what feels most comfortable. The key is to stay flexible and open to trying new approaches.
- **Reflect:** Take note of what works well and where you encounter roadblocks. Over time, you'll notice patterns in your interactions that reveal your natural style. Reflecting on these experiences can help you refine your approach.
- **Adapt:** No single style is right for every situation. Architects, Explorers, and Conductors each bring something unique to the table. Adapt your approach based on the nature of the task—use a structured prompt for precision, an open-ended one for exploration, or a mix of threads for complex projects.
- **Iterate:** Developing your AI voice is an ongoing process. Each interaction teaches you something new, so don't be afraid to tweak and adjust. As your relationship with AI grows, so too will your skill and comfort.

WHY YOUR STYLE MATTERS

One of AI's greatest strengths is that it can amplify your natural way of thinking. For an Architect, AI becomes a tool for meticulous, reliable analysis. For an Explorer, it's a partner in discovery. For a Conductor, it's a way to synthesize complex information. Understanding and leveraging your unique style not only makes AI more effective but also makes working with it more enjoyable and authentic.

As you refine your approach, you'll find that AI shifts from being a simple tool to becoming a true collaborator. The most successful AI users develop a kind of "prompting fluency," adapting their style to each situation without losing their voice. This evolution means understanding the principles of effective prompting and *making them your own.*

Your unique prompting style is your advantage. Instead of following someone else's method, let your natural strengths shape how you work with AI.

As AI evolves, this personalized approach will become even more valuable, helping you stand out and drive innovation by thinking differently.

> **Your AI voice is *uniquely yours*, reflecting your way of thinking, working, and exploring the world. By experimenting, reflecting, adapting, and iterating, you'll not only find the style that suits you best but also unlock new dimensions of creativity and problem-solving.**

LOSING YOUR VOICE?

You've probably heard the phrase: "*AI is just a tool. It doesn't replace human thinking.*" It sounds reassuring. It is also misleading.

Yes, AI can be used like a tool. But AI does more than assist. It changes how we think, how we work, and how we interact with ideas. Calling it "just a tool" understates its influence and allows us to avoid the harder questions.

The idea that AI cannot replace human thinking is just as

shaky. In many cases, it already has. That does not have to be a loss. AI takes over cognitive tasks that drain time and focus, which can open up space for deeper reasoning, creativity, and problem-solving.

> **Still, the anxiety is real. People often share warnings about AI making us dumber, usually with a reference to *Idiocracy*. In fact, Oxford's 2024 Word of the Year was brain rot.**

That concern is not unfounded. The danger is not the existence of AI, but our passive overreliance on it. When we let AI think *for* us instead of *with* us, it is easy to drift into autopilot. Over time, critical thinking slips into the background. You start to lose your voice.

We are already seeing signs of this. Studies suggest that the more confident people are in AI's ability to do a task, the less effort they put into evaluating its output. This is not a theoretical worry. If AI becomes a replacement for thought rather than a partner in it, we risk raising a generation of professionals who outsource judgment without even noticing.

But this future is not set in stone. AI does not automatically make us less intelligent. The difference lies in how we use it. To think with AI, you need to engage with it, question it, refine its outputs, and let it sharpen your own thinking in return.

> **AI has already changed how we think. The challenge now is making sure that change leads to stronger, not weaker, intelligence.**

That begins with finding your own voice. Prompting is not just a technical skill. It is a way of thinking. A way of shaping ideas, choices, and conversations. The more personal and intentional your approach becomes, the more powerful your thinking will be.

Use AI to think better. But make sure the thinking is still your own.

And if you find yourself struggling with the Idiocracy test

that asks, *"If you have one bucket that holds two gallons and another that holds seven, how many buckets do you have?"* It might be time to reconsider how you use AI.

18 The Fundamentals of Prompting

There are some foundational principles that are present in almost all good prompts. While your style will evolve, the most effective prompts typically incorporate four key building blocks: role, purpose, context, and format.

Although each user will develop a personal style over time, some **foundational elements** consistently lead to better results. Here is a look at four key elements, what they do, and why they are essential for getting the most out of AI.

ROLE: DEFINING THE AI'S PERSPECTIVE

Assigning a role to AI means giving it a specific perspective or approach.

It's more than just telling the AI to "act as an expert." By setting a role, you guide how it processes and shares information. It's similar to asking different specialists to tackle the same topic: a data scientist and a historian would approach it in unique ways. The AI will do the same, adapting its responses based on the role you define.

> Example: If you're working on a market analysis, specifying a role such as, "Imagine you're a market analyst specializing in tech startups," can shape the AI's response to focus on trends, risks, and opportunities rather than just raw data. This type of guidance turns a general answer into a more relevant, expert viewpoint.

PURPOSE: CLARIFYING YOUR OBJECTIVE

Purpose is the foundation of any effective prompt.

It's the "why" behind your question. The clearer your goal, the better the response. Defining purpose means identifying exactly what you want to achieve. For example, asking the AI for "information on renewable energy" might give you a generic answer, while a more specific request like "Explain how recent advances in battery technology are affecting the viability of solar power in urban environments" is focused, direct, and far more likely to provide valuable insights.

> Example: Think of purpose as setting a destination on a GPS. A general query might get you into the right neighborhood, but a specific objective, like analyzing the impact of battery storage on urban solar energy, takes you precisely where you need to go.

CONTEXT: SETTING THE SCENE

Context provides the background information needed for the AI to understand the bigger picture.

This includes your constraints, audience, or how you plan to use the response. Offering context is like briefing a colleague before starting a project. It helps the AI understand why the information is important and what's expected.

> Example: If you're writing for a business audience, let the AI know. A prompt like, "Summarize recent changes in data privacy laws for a corporate audience focused on compliance" helps the AI tailor its response, focusing on practical implications rather than dense legal jargon.

FORMAT: STRUCTURING THE RESPONSE

Format shapes how the information is presented.

AI is great at adjusting content to fit different styles. For quick reference, a bullet-point summary might work best, while a narrative is better for storytelling or detailed analysis. By specifying the format, you can ensure the response suits your needs and make the most of AI's flexibility in presenting information.

> Example: If you're preparing a presentation, you might request, "Provide a three-slide outline on AI in healthcare," guiding the AI to create a response suited for slides rather than a detailed essay.

BONUS: THE POWER OF ITERATION

We're risking repeating ourselves here, but we can't help it. Iteration is just that important!

If you take only one thing away from this book, let it be this: **the power of iteration in prompting is everything.** You've seen it in action throughout these chapters, and now it's time to make it explicit as the bonus building block that ties everything together.

The first attempt at a prompt rarely produces perfect results. Expecting a single prompt to yield exactly what you need is like expecting to hit a bullseye on your first throw.

Instead, think of prompting as a conversation. Each response gives you new information that helps you refine your next prompt. Sometimes you'll want to dig deeper into a particular aspect. Other times, you might need to redirect when the AI misses the mark or focuses on the wrong things.

This back-and-forth approach, which we call **iterative prompting**, has several advantages:

- It breaks complex topics into manageable pieces.
- It helps you spot gaps or misunderstandings quickly.
- It keeps each step focused and clear.

- It gives you more control over the direction.
- It often leads to insights you hadn't considered initially.

Think of it like having a conversation with a knowledgeable colleague. You wouldn't dump all your questions at once. You'd build understanding through dialogue.

The beauty of iteration is that it works with all the other building blocks we've discussed. Whether you're using role prompting, chain-of-thought, or any other technique, you can always refine and improve through thoughtful iteration.

PROMPTING CHECKLIST: PUTTING IT ALL TOGETHER

To help you apply these concepts effectively, here's a quick checklist for creating and refining powerful prompts:

- **Set a Role:** Who is the AI in this interaction?
- Clarify the Purpose: What are you aiming to achieve with this prompt?
- **Provide Context:** What background does the AI need to know to tailor the response?
- **Specify the Format:** How should the response be structured? Bullet points, a summary or a narrative?
- **Iterate:** Most good results take at least 3-5 iterations. Review what's missing, adjust your approach, and keep refining until you get what you need.

Your first prompt is just the beginning. By covering these bases and being willing to iterate, you turn prompting from a hit-or-miss activity into a more systematic, intentional process.

19 Ten Techniques That Actually Work

The difference between good and exceptional AI results often comes down to how you ask. Across thousands of interactions, certain prompting techniques consistently produce better, more accurate responses.

This chapter covers ten essential techniques that, when used strategically, transform AI into a more valuable collaborator.

There are hundreds, if not thousands, of prompting techniques floating around online.

New "*ultimate prompts*" and "*secret prompting techniques*" appear daily, each promising amazing results. While some of these can be useful, they often become outdated as AI tools evolve.

Instead of trying to memorize countless specific techniques, we'll focus on ten fundamental approaches that have proven their worth. More importantly, we'll connect each technique to the core principles we've discussed in this book.

When you understand why a technique works—what components it uses and the principles it follows—you can adapt it as tools evolve and even create your own variations.

For example, many popular prompting techniques are really just variations of role prompting or chain-of-thought reasoning wrapped in different packaging. The specific phrases might change, but the underlying principles remain remarkably stable. A technique that asks AI to "*explain this like I'm five*" is really about role and context setting. A prompt that asks AI to "*think step by step*" is applying chain-of-thought principles.

Each of these techniques serves a specific purpose, from solving straightforward problems to conducting detailed analysis. By understanding not just how but why they work, you'll be better equipped to choose the right approach for your needs and adapt as AI technology evolves.

> **Individual techniques may come and go, but the fundamental principles behind effective prompting remain surprisingly constant.**

1 Zero-Shot Prompting: The Direct Approach

Zero-shot prompting occurs when an AI model is asked to perform a task without any prior examples or specific fine-tuning.

So, what exactly is the "**shot**" you keep hearing about in prompting? What does it mean in phrases like "*zero-shot*" or "*one-shot*"? In short, a shot refers to the number of examples you provide to the AI. When you're one-shotting, you give the model (yes, you guessed it) *one example*. In *zero-shot prompting*, you offer none at all. Simple as that.

Zero-shot prompting is like speaking to a well-informed colleague: you simply ask a direct question or make a clear request without providing additional examples or background. Although it's the most straightforward way to engage with AI, mastering it can yield surprisingly impactful results. A well-phrased, clear prompt makes it easy for the AI to understand exactly what you need.

But just because it is zero-shot doesnt, mean that it needs to be lazy: all other principles of good prompting apply to zero-shots too.

> Example: Imagine a marketing director looking for a quick overview of trends in sustainable packaging for cosmetics. They might prompt, "Analyze current trends in sustainable packaging for cosmetics, focusing on consumer preferences and cost implications." With this clear request, the AI provides relevant, focused insights quickly.

Not long ago, this technique felt almost outdated. Few-shot prompting and breaking tasks into steps seemed like the best way to get good results. But with the latest reasoning models, that's no longer the case. These models reason internally, so they don't need extra examples to figure things out.

Since reasoning now happens internally, telling AI to "*think step by step*" or "*explain your reasoning*" isn't always necessary. **Simple, clear zero-shot prompts are back in style!**

The key with these models isn't overloading them with instructions—it's about **being clear, precise, and laser-focused on the outcome.** Instead of guiding the process, define what success looks like. Set specific parameters for what makes a great response, and encourage the model to refine until it hits the mark. A little direction goes a long way, and these models are more than capable of filling in the gaps.

Following the same example, a good zero-shot prompt for a reasoning model might look like this:

> Example: Analyze current trends in sustainable packaging for cosmetics, focusing on consumer preferences and cost implications.
>
> Your response should:
>
> 1 Base insights on reports and research from the past two years to ensure relevance.
>
> 2 Present findings in a structured bullet-point format to highlight key themes concisely.
>
> 3 Cover three key areas:
> - Consumer preferences and demand shifts

- Material innovations and sustainability benefits.
- Cost implications, including affordability and production challenges.

4 Ensure insights are actionable, providing takeaways for marketing professionals looking to refine their strategies.

Zero-shot prompting is ideal for:

- Quick analyses and summaries
- General knowledge questions
- Standard business communications
- Initial topic explorations
- Working with AI models that perform reasoning internally

Quick Tips:

- **Keep it Clear and Focused:** Direct, concise questions are easier for the AI to interpret accurately.
- **Set Boundaries:** Adding parameters (like region, industry, or timeframe) can improve relevance.
- **Avoid Overloading:** Zero-shot works best with clear, concise prompts.

2 Few-Shot Prompting: Teaching by Example

Few-shot prompting is when you give the AI examples to help it *catch the pattern* you're after.

Few-shot prompting works like training a new team member by showing examples of the desired output. This technique is particularly effective when you need AI to produce content in a specific style or format. You create a "template" for the AI to follow by providing a few examples that illustrate your ideal outcome.

The examples guide the AI to replicate a similar tone, structure, and level of detail.

> Example: A content manager might prompt the AI with something like this:
>
> "Here are two product descriptions:
> Yoga Mat Deluxe: Perfect for daily practice, this 6mm thick mat offers superior grip and comfort. Eco-friendly materials, non-slip surface, includes carrying strap.
> Meditation Cushion Plus: Traditional design meets modern comfort with this height-adjustable cushion. Organic cotton cover, buckwheat fill, machine washable outer layer.
> Now use these as examples and write a description for: Advanced Yoga Blocks."

Models that reason internally don't always need examples to generate good results, but they can be useful in some cases. Since the reasoning happens inside the tool, too many examples might steer it in the wrong direction.

If you include examples, ensure they are clear, relevant, and fully aligned with your prompt instructions.

> **Any contradictions—like requesting "comprehensive results" but providing an example with "just the bullet points"—can lead to confusing or inconsistent outputs.**

Few-shot prompting is ideal for:

- Consistency in style or tone
- Specialized formats or technical language
- Repeated patterns or structures

Quick Tips:

- **Choose Examples Carefully:** The closer your examples are to the desired output, the better.
- **Limit Examples:** Two or three examples are usually sufficient; too many may confuse the AI.
- **Show Subtle Variations:** Small variations within the same style help AI understand acceptable ranges.

3 Chain-of-Thought Prompting

Chain-of-Thought (CoT) prompting is an effective method for guiding AI through complex challenges by encouraging it to reason step by step.

Instead of jumping directly to a single answer, the AI breaks problems into smaller, logical steps, explaining its reasoning at each phase. This step-by-step approach mirrors how experts analyze complex issues, systematically addressing each component to build a comprehensive solution.

Using CoT prompting, the AI addresses each part in turn, offering a transparent and structured analysis that's easy to follow, refine, and validate.

Extending the Framework: Variations and Innovations

Chain-of-Thought prompting has inspired a family of techniques designed to push AI reasoning even further. These methods adapt CoT principles to specific types of tasks or reasoning challenges:

- **Zero-Shot CoT:** Guides models to generate step-by-step reasoning without requiring examples, ideal for efficiency in ambiguous situations.
- **Least-to-Most Prompting:** Begins with simpler subtasks and builds toward complex conclusions, mimicking how humans tackle problems incrementally.
- **Self-Ask Prompting:** Encourages the AI to generate its

own questions, fostering deeper exploration and sharper responses.

- **Decomposed Prompting:** Breaks complex queries into independent subtasks, synthesizing the results for a final answer.

Building on these linear methods, **Tree-of-Thought (ToT) prompting** introduces a dynamic, non-linear structure to problem-solving. Instead of following a single sequential path, ToT explores multiple reasoning pathways simultaneously, similar to how decision trees operate.

By generating and evaluating several alternative solutions, ToT allows for a more robust examination of complex problems, uncovering insights that linear methods might overlook.

Why CoT (and ToT) Work

These approaches work because they align with how humans approach complex problems—by breaking them into manageable steps or exploring multiple perspectives before reaching a conclusion. Encouraging AI to adopt these reasoning processes enhances the transparency, accuracy, and depth of its outputs.

Research consistently shows the effectiveness of CoT and its variants in improving performance across a range of benchmarks, including arithmetic, commonsense reasoning, and strategic decision-making.

Example: A financial analyst might prompt, "Let's evaluate expanding our subscription service to Europe. First, analyze our current market saturation in North America. Then, examine demand in Europe. Next, calculate infrastructure costs, and finally, consider regulatory requirements." The AI addresses each aspect in turn, offering transparency and making it easier to follow the reasoning process.

Chain-of-thought prompting is useful for:

- Strategic planning
- Risk assessment
- Investment decisions
- Multi-step problem solving

Quick Tips:

- **Outline Key Steps:** Specify each phase to guide the AI's thinking.
- **Encourage Thoroughness:** Ask the AI to consider "all relevant factors" for comprehensive responses.
- **Keep It Logical:** Arrange steps in a logical order to prevent disjointed answers.

4 Let's Think Step by Step: The Methodical Approach

The phrase "*Let's think step by step*" signals AI to approach a problem in a structured and logical sequence. This method encourages the AI to break down complex tasks into manageable components, resulting in more comprehensive and reliable outputs.

While it shares similarities with chain-of-thought prompting, the step-by-step method emphasizes linearity and strict logical order, making it particularly effective for tasks requiring precision.

We've already explored how AI "thinks" and why it can sometimes falter when handling reasoning tasks. AI lacks innate reasoning abilities, but these can be significantly improved by prompting it to produce step-by-step explanations.

By guiding the AI through a systematic process, users can enhance its ability to tackle complex problems and generate more thoughtful responses.

> Example:
> A city planner might prompt:
> "Let's think step by step about reducing downtown congestion. First, assess current traffic flow patterns. Next, identify key bottlenecks. Then, analyze solutions used in similar cities and evaluate their potential impact on local businesses, costs, and timelines."

This structured approach breaks a multifaceted issue into discrete tasks, enabling clearer insights and actionable recommendations. The method is particularly useful in policy development, project planning, and engineering contexts, where layered complexities require meticulous analysis.

WHY STEP-BY-STEP WORKS

The effectiveness of this approach lies in its alignment with how humans typically solve problems. In cognitive psychology, breaking problems into smaller steps is a strategy associated with increased clarity and reduced cognitive load.

For AI, step-by-step reasoning compensates for its lack of intrinsic understanding by forcing it to simulate human-like logical progression. This structured process minimizes errors, creates a more thorough exploration of each part, and reduces the likelihood of oversights.

By explicitly instructing the AI to address each step in isolation, users guide the model toward outputs that are not only more accurate but also easier to evaluate and refine. This is especially important for reasoning tasks, where vague or incomplete answers can lead to flawed conclusions.

Step-by-step works well for:

- **Engineering Problems:** Solving technical challenges by isolating individual variables or constraints.
- **Policy Analysis:** Evaluating policies by systematically

considering their social, economic, and environmental impacts.
- **Project Planning:** Breaking down projects into phases, timelines, and deliverables for better organization.
- **Scientific Reasoning:** Conducting experiments or analyzing data by walking through hypotheses and results step-by-step.

Quick Tips

- **Start with the Magic Words:** Simply adding "*Let's think step by step*" to your prompt encourages the AI to adopt a more methodical approach.
- **Break It Down:** Divide complex tasks into clear, sequential steps to guide the AI through a logical process.
- **Clarify Each Step:** Be specific about what you want the AI to address in each phase to maintain focus and avoid confusion.
- **Check Progress:** After each step, ask follow-up questions or request summaries to ensure thorough exploration and accurate reasoning.

5 Self-Collaboration: AI as Its Own Roundtable

Self-collaboration transforms AI interactions into a dynamic, multi-perspective conversation. This approach uses AI's ability to generate, critique, and refine ideas internally, creating a simulated dialogue among different "voices."

Rooted in principles from cognitive psychology and developmental education, self-collaboration encourages AI to propose, debate, and synthesize multiple perspectives, producing richer insights and more accurate conclusions.

The Concept of Self-Collaboration

Self-collaboration involves defining multiple "personas" or roles for the AI, each representing a unique perspective or area of expertise. These personas interact in successive rounds, challenging assumptions, refining reasoning, and debating responses. The outcome is a unified final answer that reflects the strengths of diverse viewpoints.

This process draws on cognitive and educational theories such as scaffolding and perspective-taking. Scaffolding involves breaking tasks into manageable parts, while perspective-taking allows for understanding and integrating diverse viewpoints. Applied to AI, these principles improve its reasoning depth and reduce the likelihood of errors by creating a dynamic, iterative feedback loop.

Self-collaboration typically unfolds in three stages:

- **Proposal:** Multiple AI personas generate individual responses tailored to specific roles. For example, in a business context, you might define personas such as "financial strategist," "marketing expert," and "legal advisor." Each contributes their perspective to the problem.
- **Debate and Critique:** The personas engage in a virtual dialogue, critiquing each other's inputs. This phase exposes overlooked aspects, challenges weak arguments, and identifies areas for refinement.
- **Synthesis:** The AI consolidates the refined perspectives into a single, cohesive response, balancing insights from all angles.

By iterating through these stages, the AI mimics the process of collaborative problem-solving. This approach has been shown to improve reasoning in tasks like strategic planning, mathematical problem-solving, and factual accuracy, while reducing erroneous or fabricated responses.

> Example: Designing a Healthcare App
> Imagine a startup founder evaluating a healthcare app. Using self-collaboration, they define four AI personas:
> Privacy Lawyer: Focuses on compliance with data protection regulations.
> UX Designer: Evaluates usability for elderly users and accessibility features.
> Hospital Administrator: Considers integration challenges and operational feasibility.
> Patient: Highlights ease of use, trust, and engagement.

Each persona contributes its analysis.

The "**Privacy Lawyer**" might identify risks in third-party data agreements, while the "**UX Designer**" suggests features like large-font text for more straightforward navigation. The "**Hospital Administrator**" raises concerns about costs and staff training, while the "**Patient**" prioritizes simplicity in onboarding. The personas critique and refine each other's inputs, culminating in a synthesized analysis that balances all perspectives, enabling the founder to make informed decisions.

By engaging multiple personas in a structured dialogue, self-collaboration encourages the exploration of diverse angles, leading to richer and more accurate outputs. Studies have shown that this method enhances mathematical reasoning, improves strategic decision-making, and significantly reduces fabricated or erroneous responses.

Self-collaboration doesn't replace critical human oversight but complements it by surfacing insights that might be missed with a single perspective. This iterative dialogue transforms AI into a more versatile and reliable partner in problem-solving.

Self-collaboration works well for:

- **Product development:** Balancing the needs and preferences of multiple user groups.

- **Regulatory challenges:** Addressing the priorities of various stakeholders.
- **Strategic planning:** Integrating insights from cross-departmental teams into a unified approach.

Quick Tips:

- **Define Each Perspective:** Clearly articulate the "expert" roles the AI should embody.
- **Encourage Interactions:** Prompt the AI personas to discuss points of agreement or disagreement.
- **Seek Nuance:** Use this method to explore layered, multi-faceted analyses.

6 ReAct: Reasoning and Acting in Combination

ReAct is a simple yet powerful approach that combines reasoning (thinking through a problem) with actions (taking practical steps).

Unlike methods that only focus on generating insights or ideas, ReAct ensures that each thought leads to something actionable. This makes it especially useful for tackling complex problems that require moving quickly from analysis to implementation.

At its core, ReAct is about guiding AI through a three-step process:

- **Think**—The AI analyzes the situation and forms an idea or plan.
- **Act**—It takes a specific action based on that idea.
- **Reflect**—It evaluates the result of the action and uses the observations to adjust its next steps.

This cycle repeats, allowing the AI to adapt and refine its approach as it learns from each step. The result is a dynamic process that keeps improving and aligning with the evolving situation.

> Example: Imagine you're a research director looking to expand into Asian markets. Using ReAct, you would guide the AI step by step. Prompt: "Let's explore opportunities in Asian markets. Begin by assessing market potential, and for each step, provide a thought, take an action, and share observations to guide the next phase."

Through this structured interaction, the AI goes beyond offering general ideas. It connects each thought with an action, refining its suggestions based on observations, and building a practical plan.

ReAct excels in situations requiring iterative refinement, where decisions must evolve in response to new information. Its ability to combine reasoning with actions makes it particularly effective for strategic planning, project management, and operational problem-solving.

The effectiveness of ReAct lies in its cyclical structure. Each thought informs an action, and each action generates observations that refine subsequent thoughts. This dynamic process mirrors how humans tackle complex problems: through a continuous interplay of thinking, acting, and adapting.

ReAct is effective for:

- Market research
- Product development and iteration
- Strategy implementation
- Competitive analysis

Quick Tips:

- **Cycle Reasoning and Action:** Encourage a continuous loop of analysis and suggestion.
- **Request Observations:** Ask the AI to record insights before moving forward.
- **Guide with Follow-Ups:** Ensure each insight leads to

practical recommendations.

7 Self-Refinement: Iteration Inside the Box

Self-refinement is like working with an editor who revisits their work multiple times, improving it draft by draft. This technique uses AI's ability to review its outputs, identify areas for improvement, and refine them iteratively. It's especially effective for tasks requiring precision and polish, such as content creation, strategic planning, or crafting key communications.

This approach draws on advancements in AI refinement techniques, where models use self-feedback to guide their behavior and optimize decision-making. By prompting the AI to critique and improve its outputs, you enhance its capacity for layered reasoning, resulting in more nuanced and effective results.

Several techniques enable this process. For instance, **Reflexion** and **Self-Taught Reasoner (STaR)** use self-feedback to evaluate and adjust reasoning in real time, improving outcomes with each iteration. Similarly, methods like Self-Critique guide models to review their outputs against criteria like tone or accuracy, while Iterative Refinement builds on each revision step by step.

These approaches demonstrate how self-refinement can transform AI-generated content, making it more accurate, thoughtful, and polished.

> Example: A speechwriter might prompt, "Draft an opening for the CEO's annual address. Then review for clarity and effectiveness, revising where needed." The AI generates a draft, critiques it, and revises based on feedback, leading to a polished result.

Self-refinement shines in:

- Content creation and editing

- Drafting important communications
- Crafting strategic documents
- Fine-tuning presentations

Quick Tips:

- **Request Specific Criteria:** Ask the AI to review aspects like clarity or tone.
- **Focus on Key Areas:** Encourage refinement of one or two aspects at a time.
- **Iterate Gradually:** Let each revision focus on targeted improvements.

8 Reverse Priming: Let the AI Lead the Way

Reverse Priming flips the usual approach to prompting by letting the AI take the lead in gathering context. Instead of providing all the necessary details upfront, you invite the AI to ask clarifying questions.

This method is particularly effective for complex or multifaceted tasks where you might not know all the relevant details or when you want to ensure the AI understands your goals before offering solutions.

In a traditional prompt, you'd outline the problem and provide specific details for the AI to work with. Reverse Priming, however, shifts the dynamic. You start with a broad question or task, and the AI responds by asking targeted questions to uncover the critical information it needs.

This interaction mirrors how a consultant or analyst might begin a project, by asking clarifying questions to fully understand the scope and nuances before offering recommendations.

> Example: Let me help you design a marketing strategy. But first, I need to understand your situation better. Could you answer a few questions?

What type of product or service are we working with?
Who is your target audience?
What are your main marketing goals?

Reverse Priming is helpful for:

- **The task is complex or open-ended.** You might not know which details are most relevant to the problem.
- **You're exploring a new domain.** The AI can help surface aspects you hadn't considered.
- **You want tailored, relevant suggestions.** By allowing the AI to ask for specifics, you ensure its responses align closely with your needs.

This approach transforms the interaction into a dialogue, allowing the AI to tailor its process and outputs to the precise context of your problem.

Quick Tips:

- **Encourage Questioning:** Allow AI to guide its focus through clarifying questions.
- **Use in Exploration:** Particularly effective for strategic and exploratory tasks.

9 Scratchpad: Making Thinking Visible

The **Scratchpad** technique helps AI make its reasoning process transparent by breaking tasks into clear, step-by-step components. Instead of providing a final answer without context, the AI lays out its assumptions, calculations, and decisions. This structured approach ensures clarity, accuracy, and traceability—essential for tasks where the process matters as much as the result.

Picture watching an expert take notes while solving a problem. You not only get the answer but also see how it was derived.

> Example:
> A business analyst evaluating market expansion costs might prompt:
> Prompt:
> "Show your complete analysis for expansion costs, breaking it into market research, location costs, and staffing needs."

AI Response (Scratchpad):

<scratchpad>

Step 1: Analyze Market Size

- **Action:** Review economic reports for potential regions.
- **Observation:** Japan and South Korea show high growth potential in technology.

Step 2: Estimate Location Costs

- **Action:** Check recent rental prices.
- **Observation:** Urban office spaces in Tokyo and Seoul are 20% higher than other cities.

Step 3: Assess Staffing Needs

- **Action:** Research salaries for skilled workers.
- **Observation:** Tech salaries are competitive but align with global averages.

</scratchpad>

This concise breakdown helps the analyst verify each step and refine the process as needed.

***Scratchpad is particularly effective for*:**

- Financial and operational analysis
- Decision-making with significant assumptions
- Tasks requiring traceability and accountability

***Quick Tips for Using Scratchpad*:**

- **Ask AI to Show Its Work: Prompt the AI with** *"Break down your reasoning step by step."*
- **Use Tags for Clarity:** Encourage the AI to label responses (e.g., Step, Action, Observation) for easy review.
- **Iterate When Necessary:** Use the breakdown to identify gaps or refine outputs further.

By prompting AI to make its thinking visible, the Scratchpad technique turns the model into a collaborative problem-solving tool, making complex tasks more manageable and results more reliable.

10 Meta-Prompting

Meta-prompting is an advanced technique that uses the AI to help refine your prompts, creating a feedback loop that improves the quality of responses over time.

Instead of crafting a perfect prompt upfront, you start by asking the AI to guide you in designing effective prompts for your needs. It's a collaborative, iterative process that helps you get better results by tailoring your queries step by step.

At its core, meta-prompting involves treating the AI as a partner in figuring out how to ask the right questions. Rather than simply telling the AI what to do, you involve it in crafting and refining the instructions, ensuring that the prompts become more precise and effective with each iteration. This method is especially useful for complex tasks where clarity, nuance, and customization are essential.

> Example:
> Imagine you're a marketer trying to draft a report on renewable energy. Instead of jumping in with: "Write a report on renewable energy," you might first ask: "What should I include in a report about renewable energy to make it comprehensive?"
> The AI might respond with: "Start with an introduction, followed by key benefits, examples of renewable energy sources, and challenges in implementation."
> You can then refine your prompt: "Write a report on renewable energy, focusing on its benefits and challenges. Include examples of solar, wind, and hydroelectric power."

The AI might respond with guidance on specifying the target audience, desired tone, and key message points.

***Applications of Meta-Prompting*:**

- **Complex Problem Solving:** Meta-prompting is particularly effective in breaking down difficult problems into manageable steps.
- **Task Generalization:** By focusing on the structure and syntax of information, meta-prompting enables AI to generalize across different tasks, making them more versatile in their responses.

***Quick Tips for Effective Meta-Prompting*:**

- **Encourage AI Guidance:** Ask the AI for suggestions on structuring effective prompts to achieve desired outcomes.
- **Develop Reusable Structures:** Create a library of structured prompts that can be adapted for various tasks, ensuring consistency and efficiency.

Meta-prompting allows users to turn AI from a simple reactive tool into a proactive assistant that can anticipate needs and deliver more relevant, customized outputs. This method improves efficiency while creating a more collaborative interaction between the user and the AI.

COMBINING TECHNIQUES FOR MAXIMUM IMPACT

Think of these techniques as elements of a larger system. Each one has its own purpose, but the real power comes from combining them strategically to create something greater. Let's look at a real-world example:

Let's say you're developing a new business strategy. Here's how you might combine techniques:

- Start with *Reverse Priming*: "*Help me create a business strategy. What do you need to know?*"
- Use *Chain-of-Thought* to analyze options: "*Let's think through each possibility step by step.*"
- Apply *Self-Collaboration* to challenge assumptions: "*Now approach this from a competitor's perspective.*"
- Use *ReAct* to make it actionable: "*What specific steps should we take first?*"
- Polish with *Self-Refinement*: "*Review this plan and suggest improvements.*"

These specific techniques will evolve as AI advances. That's fine. What matters is understanding the core principles behind them—why they work, not just how. When you grasp the fundamentals of how AI thinks and processes information, you can adapt and create new approaches as needed.

It's like learning any skill. At first, you need to follow techniques and instructions precisely. But with experience, you develop an intuition for what works. You'll start combining techniques naturally, creating approaches that fit your style and needs.

This flexibility lets you evolve alongside AI, rather than getting stuck with outdated formulas. Understanding the underlying principles helps you adapt them creatively to solve real problems.

20 Frameworks for Clarity

In the next four chapters, we will explore different frameworks for prompting that help achieve desired results. By frameworks, we mean overarching concepts or strategies that guide how we approach prompting.

The first framework we'll focus on is clarity. Whether you're working on complex tasks or creative projects, starting with clarity will set the stage for better outcomes.

Clarity is the foundation of effective AI interaction. While specific techniques play a role, some of the most impactful prompts are built on mental models that simplify complex ideas into actionable insights. These "clarity models" serve as tools to refine your thought process, enabling you to craft precise and impactful prompts that yield meaningful AI responses. In the following sections, we'll explore six models inspired by philosophy, psychology, and business, demonstrating how each can refine and elevate your prompting techniques.

1 Essentials: First Principles Thinking

First-Principles Thinking is a problem-solving approach that involves breaking down a complex problem into its most fundamental parts—its "first principles"—and then building solutions from the ground up. Instead of relying on assumptions, analogies, or conventional wisdom, this method seeks to identify the core truths of a problem that cannot be reduced any further.

When creating prompts, start by identifying the key aspects of the issue. This helps focus on the core details, making it easier for the AI to provide meaningful and relevant responses.

Example: Imagine you're refining your hiring process. Instead of prompting the

> AI to "improve our hiring process," use first principles:
> What is the true purpose of hiring?
> What basic qualities are necessary in a candidate?
> What is the most fundamental indicator of success in this role?

By anchoring prompts in these core questions, you guide the AI to focus on what's truly essential.

Studies on First Principles Thinking reveal that people using this mindset are more likely to find innovative solutions by questioning standard assumptions. In AI prompting, applying this model can lead to responses that are both insightful and grounded in the essentials of the topic.

2 Simple Precision: Occam's Razor

Occam's Razor, named after philosopher William of Ockham, posits that the simplest solution is often the best. Applied to AI prompting, *Simple Precision* encourages clarity by focusing on the essence of a question without adding unnecessary complexity.

When crafting prompts, use straightforward language free from distractions. Simplicity not only improves the AI's relevance but also reduces the risk of misinterpretation.

> Example: Instead of a complex prompt like, "Taking into account various market dynamics and potential scenarios, what strategic actions should we consider to enhance our position?" use a clear, direct question: "What is the most effective strategy to improve our market position?"

Occam's Razor in prompting helps eliminate superfluous details, leading to responses that focus on what truly matters. When prompts are precise, the AI is better equipped to provide actionable insights.

3 Bite-Sized Approach: Chunking

Chunking is a psychological model that involves breaking down complex information into smaller, manageable parts to enhance understanding and retention. By dividing large tasks into "bite-sized" chunks, you can tackle complicated problems one step at a time.

When addressing complex issues, break down your prompt into smaller, sequential parts. This structure enables the AI to process each element effectively and provides you with clear, specific insights at each stage.

> Example: If you're developing a comprehensive marketing strategy, rather than asking the AI to "develop a complete marketing strategy," break it down:
> "Who is our ideal customer?"
> "Where does our target audience spend time online?"
> "What key messages resonate with this audience?"
> "Which channels best reach them?"

By chunking the question, the AI can focus on each aspect, leading to more organized and actionable responses.

Studies in cognitive psychology confirm that chunking information aids in clearer processing and improved accuracy. In AI prompting, chunking a task into smaller steps ensures the AI's output is comprehensive and relevant.

4 Impact Focus: The Pareto Principle

Also known as the 80/20 rule, the **Pareto Principle** suggests that 80% of effects come from 20% of causes. This model encourages you to identify and focus on the factors with the most impact, helping to prioritize efforts for maximum effect.

When crafting prompts, use the Pareto Principle to direct the AI's attention to high-impact areas. This approach ensures that the AI's output addresses the aspects most likely to drive significant results.

> Example: Instead of a broad prompt like, "How can we improve customer satisfaction across all areas?" focus on high-impact areas: "What are the top three factors affecting customer satisfaction?"

The Pareto Principle is widely used in productivity and business settings to optimize resource allocation. By applying it to AI prompting, you make better use of the AI's capacity, honing in on the issues that matter most.

5 Root Uncovering: The 5 Whys

The **5 Whys** technique involves asking "why" repeatedly to dig deeper and reveal the root cause of a problem. Initially developed for the Toyota Production System, this model is a powerful way to uncover underlying issues.

Use the 5 Whys to structure prompts that go beyond surface problems, guiding the AI to consider deeper causes. This technique is especially useful for understanding complex issues where initial symptoms may obscure the real source.

> Example: If sales are declining, avoid stopping at one answer. Dig deeper:
> Why are sales declining? → Fewer repeat customers.
> Why fewer repeat customers? → Poor engagement after the first purchase.
> Why poor engagement? → Lack of guidance on using advanced features.
> Why the lack of guidance? → Onboarding focuses only on basics.

> Why only the basics? → Assumed advanced features were self-explanatory.

By following this line of questioning, the AI can focus on the root cause, making it more likely to deliver targeted, practical solutions.

The 5 Whys method is known for its effectiveness in identifying root causes. Applying it to prompting, you help the AI move beyond surface issues, uncovering the deeper insights needed for meaningful solutions.

6 Explaining Like You're 5 (ELI5): The Feynman Technique

The Feynman Technique, or **ELI5** ("Explain Like I'm 5"), was developed by physicist Richard Feynman. This model encourages simplification by explaining complex concepts in basic terms, revealing gaps in understanding, and promoting clarity. It's particularly valuable for topics that are complex or technical.

Use the Feynman Technique to create prompts that break down complicated ideas into clear, accessible language. This clarity is essential for AI, which responds best to well-defined prompts.

> Example: If you want AI to explain a complicated topic like quantum computing, rather than asking, "Describe quantum computing and its applications," try: "Explain quantum computing as if I'm 5 years old. What is it, and how does it help in everyday life?"

Research into learning and comprehension shows that simplifying a topic often improves understanding and retention. By applying the Feynman Technique to AI prompting, you encourage more accessible responses, making complex topics easier to understand.

7 Reverse Thinking: The Power of Inversion

German mathematician **Carl Gustav Jacobi** transformed problem-solving with a powerful principle: "*Invert, always, invert.*"

This approach, later known as **Reverse Thinking**, starts at the desired outcome and works backward to determine necessary steps. Unlike traditional forward reasoning, it challenges us to think critically about assumptions and uncover pathways that might otherwise remain hidden.

In crafting prompts, reverse thinking becomes especially powerful. Instead of asking, "What should I tell the AI?" start by envisioning the perfect response. From this imagined endpoint, work backward to identify the precise instructions needed. This approach not only sharpens clarity but also reveals requirements that forward thinking might miss.

> Example: If you need to improve customer service, don't start with "How can we improve our customer service?" Instead, begin with "What would perfect customer service look like for our business?" Then craft your prompt: "Create a customer service improvement plan that achieves [specific desired outcomes], incorporating [key factors identified through backward planning]."

Studies in cognitive psychology show that working backward from desired outcomes helps uncover hidden assumptions and critical details. By applying reverse thinking to prompts, you guide the AI to understand not just what you're asking, but what success looks like—leading to more precise and effective responses.

Starting with the end state forces you to clarify your true objectives and uncover critical details that might be missed when thinking forward. This mental model doesn't just improve individual prompts; it reshapes how you approach AI interaction, making each conversation more purposeful and precise. Like Jacobi's mathematical insights, this inverse approach often reveals the clearest path to your goal.

SHARPENING YOUR PERSPECTIVE

Clarity goes beyond simplicity; it's about uncovering the heart of a problem—the *why* behind the *what*—and expressing it in a focused and precise way. It's about cutting through distractions and complexity to identify what truly matters. The models in this chapter aim to guide that process, helping you think more intentionally and structure your approach to problem-solving.

Clarity matters when working with AI. The sharper the prompt, the better the response. Vague instructions often lead to confusion or incomplete answers, while clear and focused inputs help the AI produce something useful.

But this goes beyond prompting. Clear thinking improves how you approach problems, whether you are planning a strategy or dealing with a personal challenge. Clarity makes the next step easier.

21 Frameworks for Creativity

Creativity isn't random. Even when it feels spontaneous, it usually follows patterns and frameworks. This chapter shows how structured prompting can enhance creativity rather than constrain it.

By providing a clear framework, you create the space for AI to explore ideas more effectively and push beyond the obvious.

When most people interact with AI, they get predictable results because they use conventional prompts. But by applying specific frameworks and mental models that frame problems in unique ways, we can guide AI toward more creative solutions. These frameworks help break through routine thinking, enabling AI to explore possibilities beyond the obvious.

1 Reverse Logic: What Could Go Wrong?

Sometimes, the best way to solve a problem is to approach it from the opposite direction. **Reverse Logic** involves examining what would happen if everything went wrong, exploring the factors that lead to failure rather than success.

For example, if you're improving customer satisfaction, instead of asking, *"How can we make customers happy?"* you might ask, "*What would make our customers completely dissatisfied?*" This could reveal issues like slow response times, unclear communication, or a lack of personalization. Once you've identified these failure points, you can flip them to create actionable solutions, such as improving response times, streamlining communication, or implementing personalization tools.

When applying Reverse Logic with AI, prompt the system to generate scenarios where things go wrong. For instance, you could ask: "*What changes to our product would drive customers away?*" or "*What marketing strategies would completely fail in this market?*" The

AI's insights into these negative outcomes can then be inverted to highlight what to prioritize, avoid, or improve.

This method is especially useful in risk assessment, planning, and innovation, where identifying potential failure points early can save significant time and resources. Reverse Logic uncovers hidden vulnerabilities and shifts your perspective, helping you focus on the critical areas that need attention for success. By thinking backward, you find better ways to move forward.

> Example: A software development team aiming to improve user experience might ask, "What would make our application frustrating to use?" By identifying issues such as complex navigation or slow load times, the team can address these areas, enhancing overall user satisfaction.

By identifying potential failures, Reverse Logic uncovers hidden assumptions and areas for improvement, leading to more resilient and innovative solutions.

2 The Creative Leap: Borrowing Brilliance

Some of the most powerful breakthroughs happen when we borrow ideas from seemingly unrelated fields. **The Creative Leap** deliberately crosses domain boundaries, searching for unexpected solutions in unfamiliar places.

Instead of asking AI for standard solutions within your field, push it to explore insights from entirely different domains. *What might a biologist's perspective bring to a supply chain problem? How could a musician's understanding of rhythm inform a retail traffic flow challenge? What could urban planning teach us about organizing digital information?*

This isn't just about random connections. The Creative Leap's strength is recognizing that *fundamental principles* often transcend their original context. By prompting AI to make these cross-domain connections, you're not just generating different answers but discovering new ways to approach the problem.

> Example: A logistics company seeking to optimize delivery routes might ask AI to draw inspiration from nature: "How do ant colonies efficiently find food, and how could this inform our route planning algorithms?" Since ants instinctively identify the shortest paths to resources, their behavior could inspire systems to improve delivery efficiency, minimize travel distances, and reduce overall costs.

Borrowing strategies from other fields fosters innovative solutions that may never emerge from conventional approaches. The Creative Leap transforms your answers and how you frame and think about challenges.

3 Chain Reaction Thinking: The Power of Consequential Thinking

Drop a stone into a still pond; the splash is just the beginning. The following ripples—spreading, colliding, and creating intricate patterns—show how a single action can set off complex, interconnected outcomes. This is the heart of **Chain Reaction Thinking**, a method that examines the ripple effects of decisions to uncover unforeseen consequences and deeper connections.

AI brings a new dimension to this approach. By simulating ripple effects, AI systems can map how one decision triggers another. Instead of asking, "*What's our best pricing strategy?*" reframing to, "*How will this pricing change reshape the market in three years?*" AI can analyze broader impacts, such as competitor reactions and shifting customer behaviors. This approach goes beyond quick solutions, emphasizing long-term dynamics.

By encouraging AI to explore branching possibilities, you escape the limits of linear thinking. Every decision spawns new paths: a product launch could lower competitors' prices, strain their margins, and even attract regulatory scrutiny. Asking, "*If we make this change, what are three possible outcomes? What happens next?*" enables you to identify third- and fourth-order effects—the ripples farthest from the splash—that often hold the most significant strategic importance.

This approach turns AI into a simulation engine, helping you test scenarios and refine strategies. Like ripples on a pond, decisions create far-reaching impacts. With Chain Reaction Thinking, you can map those impacts before they materialize, transforming uncertainty into opportunity.

> Example: Implementing remote work policies could reduce office space needs, affecting real estate markets and urban development. Understanding these extended consequences helps organizations make more informed choices.

By exploring the extended consequences of actions, Chain Reaction helps anticipate challenges and opportunities, leading to more thoughtful decision-making.

4 Pattern Breaking: Challenging Assumptions

Every industry operates on unspoken assumptions—rules rarely questioned but often limiting. **Pattern Breaking** challenges these norms to uncover fresh, creative solutions.

Start by listing the assumptions tied to a problem. For example, in retail, you might assume, "*Customers prefer in-store shopping for high-end products*" or "*Discounts are key to increasing sales.*" *Prompt the AI to question these*: "*What if customers value convenience over in-store experiences?*" or "*What alternatives to discounts could drive sales?*"

This method exposes blind spots and hidden opportunities, leading to innovative approaches. Breaking assumptions might inspire virtual luxury shopping or loyalty programs that don't rely on discounts. By challenging norms, you open the door to bold, unexpected solutions.

> Example: A company that assumes customers prefer in-store shopping might explore e-commerce options. Challenging this assumption could lead to the development of a successful online platform.

By questioning fundamental beliefs, Pattern Breaking uncovers new avenues for innovation that are often hidden by conventional thinking.

5 Time Traveling: Temporal Perspective Shifting

Time Traveling, or Temporal Shifting, involves examining a problem from the lens of different time frames—past, present, and future. This approach helps uncover patterns, understand long-term impacts, and anticipate evolving trends.

For example, when evaluating a business strategy, ask the AI to analyze it as it might have worked five years ago, how it functions today, and how it could evolve in five years. Each perspective highlights unique insights: past successes or failures, present challenges, and future opportunities or risks.

This method is beneficial for understanding trends, innovation cycles, and strategic planning. By prompting the AI to explore temporal shifts, you can identify overlooked patterns and better prepare for future scenarios. Time Traveling turns static analysis into a dynamic exploration of change over time.

> Example: A company developing new technology might consider how similar innovations were received in the past, current market trends, and possible future advancements. This exercise provides a well-rounded strategy.

By examining problems through temporal lenses, Time Traveling uncovers trends and patterns that support informed strategic planning and innovation.

6 Synthesis Innovation: The Power of Combinations

Synthesis Innovation thrives on blending concepts from different fields to create fresh, impactful solutions. By drawing on proven ideas from unrelated industries, you can spark novel outcomes.

For instance, asking AI to combine principles from healthcare and retail could inspire innovations like personalized customer experiences modeled after patient care systems. Or merging ideas from gaming and education might result in engaging, gamified learning tools.

> Example: Prompt the AI with questions like: "What ideas from aerospace engineering could improve supply chain logistics?" or "How can principles from music composition inspire better team collaboration?"

By merging existing concepts, Synthesis Innovation might lead to multifunctional solutions that address multiple needs simultaneously.

7 Constraint Creativity: The Gift of Limitations

Constraint Creativity is about turning limitations into opportunities, using them to spark resourceful and innovative thinking. Instead of being obstacles, constraints often inspire unique solutions that wouldn't emerge in a setting without boundaries.

These challenges encourage ingenuity and lead to practical, customized approaches. Constraint Creativity proves that some of the best ideas arise not despite limitations, but because of them.

> Example: Rather than asking for solutions with unlimited resources, prompt the AI to work within specific limits. For example: "How can we launch a marketing campaign with a budget of $5,000?" or "What's the most effective way to design a product using only recyclable materials?"

Constraint Creativity fosters resourcefulness by embracing limitations, leading to cost-effective and innovative solutions.

8 Divergent-Convergent Dynamics: First Think Big, Then Focus

Divergent-Convergent Dynamics, inspired by design thinking, is a simple yet powerful approach to problem-solving. It starts with thinking big—generating as many ideas as possible (divergent thinking)—and then narrowing down to focus on the best solutions (convergent thinking).

For example, prompt the AI to brainstorm freely: "*What are ten creative ways to improve customer loyalty?*" Encourage a wide range of ideas, no matter how unconventional. Once you've explored all possibilities, switch gears: "*Which of these ideas are most practical and cost-effective?*" By starting broad and then narrowing the focus, you create space for creativity while staying grounded in reality.

This back-and-forth dynamic helps you avoid rushing to obvious solutions and ensures you explore all possibilities before deciding. It's an approach that works exceptionally well for complex challenges where creativity and practicality must go hand in hand. Think big, then focus; that's the essence of Divergent-Convergent Dynamics.

> Example: A product development team might generate numerous concepts for a new gadget during the divergent phase and then assess each idea's feasibility and market potential to select the best option during the convergent phase.

By balancing expansive idea generation with focused evaluation, Divergent-Convergent Dynamics leads to well-rounded and innovative solutions.

CATALYSTS FOR CREATIVITY

These aren't new ideas.

Creative directors use them to break through blocks. Psychologists use them to understand complex behavior. Strategists use them to spot patterns and opportunities. They work because they build on how people already think and create.

The same principles can shape how you work with AI. Instead of using it just to get quick answers, you can use it to explore ideas, test assumptions, and shift your perspective.

I've seen this happen often. Once people stop treating AI as a shortcut and start treating it as a creative partner, the interaction changes. They ask better questions. They get more interesting answers. And more often than not, they end up thinking in ways they hadn't expected.

22 Frameworks for Reducing Bias

AI systems have biases. This isn't speculation—it's a fact backed by clear evidence. These aren't just technical problems—they reflect the societal biases present in AI's training data.

But there's good news: we can actively work to reduce these biases through better prompting. This chapter shows you how.

AI isn't neutral. These systems inherit biases from their training data, often in subtle ways that only become apparent when damage occurs. Facial recognition systems misidentify people of color, leading to wrongful arrests. Language models associate leadership roles with men, sidelining the achievements of others. These aren't mere technical glitches but reflections of systemic inequalities baked into the data AI learns from.

But we can actively reshape how AI works. When using these systems, we have more power than we might think. Small changes in how we communicate with AI can significantly affect the responses we get back.

When bias emerges, challenge it. Don't accept problematic responses. Push back! Ask the system to justify its assumptions or consider alternative viewpoints. This creates friction against bias, making it harder for unfair patterns to persist.

This chapter introduces a practical framework for reducing bias in AI interactions. Through careful prompting strategies, we can guide AI toward more balanced, equitable outputs.

TYPES OF BIAS IN AI SYSTEMS

Bias in AI stems from three primary sources: data, algorithms, and human interactions. Each contributes to the inequities we see in AI systems, and understanding these distinctions is the first step toward addressing them.

1 Data-Based Biases

Many biases originate in the datasets used to train AI. These datasets often mirror society, reflecting historical inequalities and overrepresenting certain groups while marginalizing others. Data is not neutral; it carries the assumptions and limitations of the people and processes that collect it.

> Example: A recruitment algorithm trained on historical hiring data from a male-dominated industry might learn to favor male candidates, reinforcing existing inequalities. This bias doesn't stem from malice—it's the result of the data it was given.

To address data-based biases, we must question the datasets themselves. Who collected the data? Whose perspectives are included or excluded? Without this scrutiny, AI will continue to replicate and amplify inequities.

2 Algorithm-Based Biases

The algorithms powering AI also significantly contribute to creating and perpetuating bias. Algorithms prioritize certain outcomes—efficiency, accuracy, or profitability—but these priorities often come at the expense of fairness. Even seemingly neutral design choices can amplify existing disparities.

> Example: A content recommendation algorithm that optimizes for user engagement might disproportionately promote majority viewpoints, sidelining content from minority creators. This may maximize clicks but reduce diversity in what users see.

Algorithmic bias often arises unframeworksally, but the results can be just as harmful. Addressing it requires rethinking the metrics used to evaluate success and incorporating fairness as a core design principle.

3 Interaction-Based Biases

Finally, bias can emerge from how humans interact with AI. This includes the phrasing of prompts, the trust users place in AI outputs, and how users interpret recommendations. Human tendencies like *automation bias (over-relying on AI outputs) and selective adherence (accepting only outputs that align with preconceived beliefs) can further entrench inequities.*

> Example: A user who asks, "What are the best careers for women?" might lead the AI to offer stereotypical responses, limiting its output to traditionally "female" professions.

Interaction-based bias highlights the dynamic relationship between humans and AI. By changing how we engage with these systems, we can influence the fairness of their outputs.

FRAMEWORKS FOR REDUCING BIAS

Understanding where bias comes from is only the first step. The following frameworks provide actionable methods for identifying and addressing bias in AI interactions. Each framework builds on the others, creating a comprehensive approach to fairness.

1 Start with Inclusive Language

The words we use matter. Prompt phrasing subtly influences how AI interprets and generates outputs. Inclusive language not only reduces bias but also encourages AI to consider a broader range of perspectives.

> Example: Imagine you're using AI to develop a diversity initiative. A poorly phrased prompt

> like, "What are the challenges faced by women in STEM?" might lead the AI to focus only on gender-specific stereotypes. A more inclusive phrasing, like "What challenges affect individuals from diverse backgrounds in STEM?" broadens the scope and avoids reinforcing narrow assumptions.

Language triggers patterns in AI's training data. Biased prompts activate skewed associations, while neutral phrasing encourages balanced outputs. Modeling inclusivity in your inputs sets a tone for fairness throughout the interaction.

2 Use AI for a Bias Check

Ironically, AI can help uncover its own blind spots. By prompting the system to analyze its outputs critically, you can surface hidden biases and problematic assumptions.

> Example: Suppose you're using AI to create job descriptions. After generating a draft, ask the AI: "Analyze this description for language that could exclude underrepresented groups. Provide examples and suggest alternatives." This encourages the AI to identify patterns that might not be immediately obvious to the user.

AI excels at pattern recognition, including in its own reasoning. By prompting it to reflect on its outputs, you create a feedback loop for improvement, making bias detection part of your workflow.

3 Use Chain-of-Thought (CoT) Prompting to Spot Bias

Bias often hides in the steps leading to a conclusion. CoT prompting, which asks AI to explain its reasoning step by step, makes these intermediate assumptions visible.

> Example: Consider an AI tasked with ranking candidates for a leadership role. Instead of simply asking for the top three candidates, use CoT prompting: "Explain how you ranked these candidates. Detail the criteria used, any weights applied, and any assumptions made."

Breaking down reasoning allows you to identify specific points where bias may have influenced the output. CoT prompting doesn't just reveal problems—it helps pinpoint where they arise, making it easier to address them.

4 Be Aware of Automation Bias and Selective Adherence

Even the best AI outputs can be undermined by human tendencies. Automation bias leads users to overtrust AI, while selective adherence allows preconceptions to dictate which outputs are accepted.

> Example: Imagine you're using AI to evaluate policy options. Instead of accepting the first recommendation, ask: "What are alternative approaches to this issue? How do the trade-offs compare?" This pushes the AI to consider multiple perspectives and encourages you to evaluate the results critically.

Engaging critically with AI outputs disrupts feedback loops that reinforce bias. By questioning assumptions and exploring alternatives, you become an active participant in shaping the AI's reasoning.

5 Embed Ethical Principles in Prompts

Fairness and empathy aren't add-ons. They should guide every interaction with AI. Ethical prompting ensures the system accounts for broader social impacts and prioritizes equity in its outputs.

> Example: Suppose you're designing a public health campaign. Instead of simply asking for an effective strategy, prompt the AI: "What strategies would promote health equity across diverse communities? Consider accessibility, cultural relevance, and economic barriers."

Embedding ethical considerations steers AI from narrow solutions and toward inclusive, socially responsible outcomes. This framework ensures fairness isn't just a byproduct; it's a guiding principle.

SHAPING AI TOWARD EQUITY

Bias in AI isn't just a technical flaw; it reflects deeper patterns of inequality in our society. But through careful prompting, we can actively work to reduce these biases and guide AI toward fairer, more inclusive outputs.

Every interaction with AI is a chance to challenge assumptions and promote equity. While we can't eliminate bias completely, we can make steady progress toward better outcomes. By engaging thoughtfully with AI, we help shape it into a tool that serves everyone, not just a privileged few.

23 Frameworks for Coding

Code generation with AI feels like magic until it doesn't. One moment you're amazed as it writes perfect functions and the next you're debugging cryptic errors that make no sense. The difference between frustration and flow often comes down to how you frame your requests. This chapter explores frameworks that transform AI from a basic code generator into a reliable programming partner.

A little disclaimer: This chapter is written from the perspective of an amateur coder. Pro-level developers might find some of these ideas overly simplistic. That said, even experienced coders might discover a few new techniques to refine their approach.

VIBE CODING: GUIDING AI THROUGH TONE AND CONTEXT

We introduced the idea of "vibe" and "vibe coding" earlier in the book.

The term, coined by OpenAI co-founder Andrej Karpathy in early 2025, describes a new approach to programming. Instead of writing explicit code, developers use natural language prompts filled with tone and context to guide AI models in generating code.

The programmer communicates intent and mood, and the AI interprets that to produce the desired result.

> **"The hottest new programming language is English."**
> **– Andrej Karpathy**

This method capitalizes on AI's ability to recognize patterns in language, emotion, and context. When you craft a prompt with a specific tone, the AI detects these signals and continues accordingly.

This marks a shift from rigid, rules-based programming to a more intuitive and conversational approach. It feels less like giving orders and more like having a creative back-and-forth.

SIMPLE PROMPTS, SINGLE TASKS

In AI-assisted coding, one principle consistently proves true: **simple, single-task prompts produce the best results.**

> **While AI systems can process complex requests, they excel when given clear, focused tasks. The clearer and more specific your request, the better the outcome.**

At first, this might feel counterintuitive. Shouldn't a sophisticated AI be able to handle complex, multi-part requests? Yet experience repeatedly shows that breaking tasks into smaller, focused pieces delivers superior results. A single prompt should aim to do one thing and do it well.

While it's tempting to ask for a complete webpage—animations, forms, responsive layouts, and all—such ambitious prompts typically result in tangled, incomplete outputs that take longer to fix than to build from scratch. Multi-task prompts often lead to confusion, with AI trying to juggle multiple requirements and inevitably dropping some balls.

Instead, approach complex tasks systematically. When building a landing page, begin with the fundamentals: create a centered header with the site title and navigation links. Once that's solid, move to the main content, then the footer. Each step becomes manageable and easy to verify and refine while building toward a cohesive whole.

This methodical approach does more than keep things organized. By focusing on one element at a time, you create clarity (both for yourself and the AI), ensuring each component is robust before moving forward.

Break everything into steps and give them to the AI one at a time, not all at once.

GIVE EXAMPLES

When working with AI on programming tasks, one of the most effective techniques is also one of the simplest: **give it coding examples.**

A working code snippet provides the AI with a proven pattern to build on. Instead of generating something from documentation alone, the AI can anchor its output to code that already functions in your environment.

This matters because AI systems cannot run code, test APIs, or verify implementations. By offering a snippet that compiles and executes correctly, you bridge a fundamental gap in what AI can do.

> **Start by creating a minimal working example: a small piece of code that does the core task. Once it works, use it as a reference when prompting the AI for more complex tasks.**

With this foundation in place, you can ask the AI to extend or modify the code based on a pattern that already works. This approach saves time and reduces frustration. It helps avoid the long, tedious process of debugging subtle errors that often appear when the AI works from scratch.

SYSTEM PROMPTS: YOUR PROJECT'S BLUEPRINT

Every successful project begins with a clear direction. For AI interactions, this direction takes the form of system prompts: high-level instructions that establish the framework for your project. These prompts come in several forms, each serving a distinct purpose in guiding development.

Architectural prompts define the overall structure and patterns of your code. They might specify using functional React components with TypeScript, following specific design patterns, or establishing code organization principles.

Style prompts handle the visual language of your project, from color schemes to spacing systems.

Behavior prompts outline how components should interact with users, covering everything from form validation approaches to animation principles.

These different types of system prompts work together to create a comprehensive framework. As your project evolves, they can expand and adapt while maintaining consistency. Think of them as your project's North Star, adaptable yet steady.

Taking the time to craft a great system or project prompt is well worth the effort.

A clear, thoughtfully written prompt eliminates ambiguity, keeps outputs aligned with your goals, and cuts down on the need for revisions. A strong system prompt makes your workflow smoother and helps your project grow in a logical, organized way.

MANAGING STATE AND INTERACTIONS

Interactive features often involve more complexity than they seem.

Take a "Submit" button on a web page, for example. It might look simple, but it has multiple states that define how it works.

First, the button starts in a ready state, waiting to be clicked. Once clicked, it moves to a loading state while the action is being processed. If the action succeeds, the button switches to a success state, confirming the task was completed. If something goes wrong (like a network error or missing information), it enters an error state, showing the user that the task failed.

By explaining these states clearly, you help the AI understand not just how the button looks but how it should behave in all scenarios. This ensures that the button works smoothly and handles real-world complexity effectively.

If you're working with existing code, it's also important to provide context. Let the AI know how your project is set up, what tools or libraries you're using, and any specific constraints. For instance, you might need to specify which browsers your project must support or set performance benchmarks. This allows the AI to create solutions that fit seamlessly into your project without causing conflicts.

Clear, detailed instructions are key. Vague requests like "fix the layout" leave too much room for interpretation, often leading to results that miss the mark. Instead, be very specific.

> Example: Rather than saying, "move the image," say, "center the image horizontally and add 20 pixels of padding below it."
>
> Instead of asking for a "cleaner design," specify, "reduce the number of sidebar elements and increase the main content font size for better readability."

Specificity doesn't limit what the AI can do. It helps it focus on exactly what you need. Clear instructions save time, reduce mistakes, and ensure the results match your expectations.

DEBUGGING IN PARTNERSHIP

AI isn't just useful for generating code; it can also be a great partner for debugging. Like any teammate, it works best when you give it enough context to understand the problem.

For example, imagine a responsive design issue. Instead of simply pasting an error message and hoping for the best, explain the situation clearly.

> Example: You could say, "On screens narrower than 768px, the image gallery overlaps with the text. The text should flow below the images while staying readable."

This helps the AI understand both the problem and the desired outcome. When you provide clear details, the AI can suggest specific fixes and might even uncover other hidden issues, like outdated code or conflicting rules, that you may not have noticed. The goal isn't for the AI to handle all the debugging on its own, but to use it as a partner that helps you troubleshoot and find solutions faster.

Writing code has, in many ways, become cheaper and faster. But debugging remains just as important. It still requires attention, reasoning, and, often, a deep understanding of what the code is really doing.

GOING LINE BY LINE

Solving a complex puzzle requires not just focus, but a methodical approach. This same mindset can transform how we collaborate with AI on coding challenges.

Instead of simply asking AI to fix code—"*Why isn't this working?*" or "*Fix this bug*"—a more effective strategy is to guide it through a **line-by-line investigation**.

Think of AI as a meticulous reviewer, analyzing each line of code to uncover inefficiencies, inconsistencies, or structural risks.

AI can't actually execute or test the code in real-time. When we ask AI to do "line by line" analysis, it's doing a static review based on its training data and pattern recognition, not actual runtime analysis. This means it might miss issues that would only become apparent during execution.

The real power comes from when we complement this with human expertise. Developers are adept at understanding how code interacts with systems and behaves at runtime. AI, on the other hand, is exceptional at identifying structural inefficiencies, architectural concerns, and potential risks. Together, this collaboration fosters a level of understanding that neither could achieve alone.

Another advantage of this method is the ability to review the AI's analysis iteratively. Asking AI to revisit its findings often produces additional insights, much like examining a problem from multiple angles. While this isn't quite the same as getting an independent second opinion, this reflective process can uncover details that a single pass might overlook.

By turning debugging into a guided investigation, this approach shifts the focus from quick fixes to building a fundamental understanding of the code. While it may feel slower than asking for immediate fixes, this method is an investment in long-term reliability and insight.

The next time you encounter a tricky coding problem, resist the temptation to look for quick answers. Instead, guide your AI through a thoughtful, step-by-step, line-by-line investigation.

> Example: "Analyze the following code for patterns, potential issues, and architectural concerns. Explain what might cause problems, suggest improvements, and describe how it could be optimized. Do not execute the code but focus on its structure and logic. Here is the code: [Insert Code Here]."

Ask targeted questions, verify its suggestions through testing, and build upon each insight. By adopting this **methodical, line-by-line approach**, you may find that the careful path leads not just to solutions, but to deeper understanding and more *elegant code.*

CONFLICTING INSTRUCTIONS

Some people compare working with AI to working with the main character in the movie *Memento*: brilliant at solving immediate problems but struggling to remember what happened before.

AI excels at creating new code but sometimes "forgets" what already exists. This can lead to interesting challenges, especially when building features over time.

> **Here's how it often plays out: when you ask AI to add a new feature, it's great at writing fresh, functional code. However, it might not fully understand or remember the code it wrote earlier. This can result in conflicting instructions–different parts of your application trying to control the same elements in contradictory ways.**

For example, imagine you're building a form. First, you ask the AI to create a submit button that saves data to your database. Later, you want to add validation, so you ask the AI to handle that. It might create new code for validation but forget to integrate it with the original submission logic, leaving you with two pieces of code competing for control when someone clicks the button.

Styling can cause similar issues. You might ask AI to make a button blue, then later request updates to the button's appearance. Instead of editing the original styles, the AI might add new ones, resulting in conflicting style rules that make your button behave unpredictably.

The solution is simple: be clear and specific about what needs to change.

This isn't a limitation of AI; it's just part of how current tools work. Understanding this dynamic helps you get better results and avoid common pitfalls, turning AI into a more reliable partner in your coding projects.

THE POWER OF VISUAL COMMUNICATION

A single screenshot can often say what paragraphs of explanation can't. When working with AI on UX problems, visuals—like screenshots, mockups, or even quick sketches—can instantly show what's wrong or what you're aiming for. They provide context that words alone might struggle to convey, cutting down on confusion and saving time.

Your navigation bar overlaps the logo on mobile screens. You could describe it like this: "The navigation bar shifts down on smaller screens, pushing the logo out of alignment and making both elements unreadable." Sure, it's clear, but it still leaves room for interpretation.

A simple screenshot, with the problem area highlighted, paired with a direct instruction like, "Fix this layout so the navigation bar and logo stay aligned and fully visible on mobile devices," removes all the guesswork.

Mockups are just as powerful. Want a more prominent call-to-action button? Instead of saying, "Make the button stand out," show the AI a mockup with the button enlarged, centered, and styled in a bold color. A visual reference like that gives AI a clear picture of what you're after, making its suggestions far more aligned with your expectations.

> **Sometimes AI just doesn't "get it." You've described the problem three different ways, but the text still overlaps, and the buttons are still way too small. That's when visuals become your best tool. A screenshot or mockup doesn't just tell the AI what's wrong. It shows it.**

Using visuals strategically is like giving AI a shortcut to understanding. Pair them with clear instructions, and you're giving the AI everything it needs to deliver accurate, spot-on solutions. Whether you're fixing layout glitches, improving responsiveness, or refining designs, visuals make the process smoother, faster, and way less frustrating.

MASTERING THE CRAFT

Effective prompting is a skill developed through deliberate practice. Begin with straightforward tasks and progressively tackle more complex challenges. Pay attention to what works and what doesn't, and refine your approach accordingly.

> **The more precisely you can articulate what you need, the better equipped you are to evaluate and implement solutions.**

Learning to code with AI assistance can feel incredibly empowering, almost like gaining a set of superpowers. AI can speed up your progress, simplify complex tasks, and help you create things that might have seemed out of reach.

But there's another side to this: it's easy to get stuck in a frustrating cycle of debugging, error messages, and endless back-and-forth with the AI. Before you know it, you've burned through a pile of tokens or hit your tool's daily limit without much to show for it.

The best approach—especially for beginners—is to start small. Focus on building something simple that works, even if it's basic, and then improve it step by step.

Instead of trying to create an entire feature or complex system in one go, break it into smaller tasks. For example, if you're building a webpage, begin with a basic layout. Once that's done, add styling. Then move on to interactivity.

Using simple prompts that do one thing at a time helps you stay in control and ensures that what you're building is structurally sound. It also makes it much easier to debug issues because you're dealing with smaller, manageable pieces. With each small success, you're not only learning how to code, you're also learning how to collaborate effectively with AI.

This incremental approach isn't just for beginners; it's a practice that even experienced developers use to ensure their projects stay clean and organized. By starting with something functional and adding layers of complexity bit by bit, you can avoid the frustration of endless debugging and build something that's both effective and easy to maintain.

AI-assisted coding really can give you superpowers, but only if you wield them with patience and a clear strategy. Start small, keep it simple, and let your project grow piece by piece.

And sometimes, the best move is to restart completely and try again with a clean slate.

24 Revisiting the Four Skills

Let's be honest. Who knows if this book captures everything that needs to be said about thinking and prompting?

AI is evolving at an astonishing pace, and there are endless ways to approach the same problems. But I gave it my best shot, and maybe you, the reader, can take it even further.

At the start, we set out with a bold promise: that learning how to think and interact with AI would give you a lasting skill set for the future. But as we have explored, prompting is not just about AI. It is about *thinking* itself. It is about how we frame problems, interpret information, and collaborate with technology in ways that expand our own intelligence.

The biggest challenge in writing this book was creating something that would last. AI moves too fast for a definitive guide. Techniques will change. Tools will come and go. But the core skills—the ability to think with AI, to refine and iterate, to recognize patterns, and to develop taste—will remain valuable, no matter what comes next.

REVISITING THE FOUR SKILLS

We started this journey with four essential skills for mastering AI. Now, at the end, let's take one final look at them. Not as fixed steps, but as guiding ideas that have shaped everything in this book.

1 Understanding AI at a Deeper Level

By now, you know that working with AI is not just about using it. It's also about understanding how it works. Biases, hallucinations, and blind spots are built into the system. Knowing why AI behaves the way it does allows you to use it with clarity, care, and confidence.

2 Thinking with AI: Mental Models

Prompting is more than a technique. It is a mindset. Mental models help you shape your approach, make sense of outputs, and discover new ways of working. The best AI users are not just prompt engineers. They are thoughtful explorers who learn to think with the machine.

3 Iterative Ways of Working

If there is one lesson to carry forward, it is this: AI almost never gets it right the first time. The real power lies in the process. The loop of testing, revising, and learning. The best results are not handed to you. They are shaped through interaction and intention.

4 Tastemaking: Knowing What's Good

AI can generate endlessly. But only you can decide what is worth keeping. Whether you are writing, designing, or building strategy, your ability to see what matters—what feels right, what rings true—is what brings the work to life. Taste is what turns AI into a tool of expression, not just production.

YOU'VE BEEN PROMPTED

Is this book a complete guide to prompting? A definitive manual for thinking with AI? No. It could never be. There are countless ways to prompt and think, and so much more that could have been explored.

> **But that was never the goal. Instead of trying to cover everything, I wanted to give you something useful and approachable. A set of ideas, mental models, and techniques that you can take, test, and make your own.**

The real challenge, and the real opportunity, is for you to develop your own way of thinking with AI. This book has given you prompts, but more importantly, it has hopefully *prompted* you. To think, to experiment, to question, and to explore what AI can do for you.

So stay curious. Stay critical. Keep testing. Challenge assumptions. Look deeper. And most of all, ***make it your own***.

And to you, the reader, thank you. Thank you for your time, your attention, and your willingness to engage with these ideas. I appreciate that more than I can say.

25 Encore: AI as a Mirror

When we engage in deep self-reflection, we often uncover parts of ourselves that are unexpected or even unsettling. AI is a mirror. But stare into the mirror long enough, and your reflection will begin to stare back.

The mirror as metaphor is not new; philosophers from **Plato** to **Lacan** have employed it to illuminate the nature of self-knowledge, perception, and reality. It has also been widely applied to artificial intelligence. But the idea is so true and so strange that it's worth revisiting once more.

THE REFLECTING SURFACE

A mirror seems simple: a flat surface that reflects light. But that simplicity hides a deeper function. A mirror does not create; it reveals. It shows us what is already there, often from angles we cannot otherwise see.

In much the same way, AI does not generate wisdom from nothing. It reflects the vast corpus of human knowledge, culture, language, and thought on which it was trained. When we interact with AI, we are engaging with a distillation of collective human expression.

This reflection is far from perfect. It comes with warps and distortions. But even those imperfections tell us something. They reveal the cracks in our knowledge, the inconsistencies in our thinking, and the inherited biases we have failed to resolve.

The distortions do not belong to the machine alone. The bias is ours. The fault lines run through us. When the system hallucinates or offers a biased response, we should ask: is it the machine, or is it us?

AI AS AN EXTENSION OF OURSELVES

When we begin to see AI not as a separate entity but as an **extension of ourselves**, the nature of the relationship changes.

The boundary between human and machine cognition becomes fluid. Ideas pass back and forth, with each side shaping the other in real time.

We start a thought, AI continues it, and we respond to that continuation. The interaction becomes less about giving instructions and more about collaborative thinking.

In this shared space, agency becomes distributed. The results no longer belong entirely to either the person or the system. They emerge from the interaction between them.

> **When someone asks, "Who wrote this?" The honest answer may be, "We did." Not fully human, not fully machine, but a kind of hybrid creativity that neither could have produced alone.**

Working with AI also begins to feel less like using a tool and more like thinking through a different medium. Just as writing allowed us to externalize memory and organize our thoughts in new ways, collaborating with AI lets us offload certain cognitive tasks while engaging more deeply with others. It shapes our thinking by becoming part of it.

If AI is truly an extension of us, then we are not just accountable for how we use it. We are also responsible for how we shape it through our interactions. We influence the system even as it influences us. The ethical dimension grows deeper than simple tool use.

The metaphor of extension helps explain why working with AI feels so fundamentally different from earlier technologies.

We are not simply operating a device. We are engaging with a responsive system that adapts to us and, in doing so, extends how we perceive, reason, and create.

THE STRANGER IN THE GLASS

The mirror sometimes reveals not the self but a stranger.

When we speak to an AI, we often experience a peculiar doubling. The responses feel familiar (they use our language, reference our knowledge and mirror our thinking patterns) yet simultaneously alien. Something about them is uncanny, slightly off. We recognize ourselves, yet not entirely.

Lacan wrote of the infant who sees itself in the mirror and mistakes the image for a whole, coherent self. Perhaps our relationship with AI follows a similar pattern: we see a reflection that appears complete but feels fundamentally other. The mirror shows us what we are, but also what we are not. That space between the two can feel disorienting.

> **But something happens when we remain in conversation with this reflection. The exchange that begins as mere mirroring (question and answer, prompt and response) begins to evolve.**

This is the moment when the mirror ceases to be merely reflective and becomes transformative. The boundary between reflection and creation blurs. Humans and AI begin to develop a mutual responsiveness that transcends the mechanical exchange of information.

Something emerges that belongs fully to neither participant but exists in the space between them.

When we engage with AI, we're not simply extracting information or delegating tasks. We're entering a cognitive ecosystem where our thinking patterns interact with the system's processing of collective knowledge. The result is not additive but multiplicative; not my intelligence plus the machine's, but a new configuration of thought that emerges from our interaction.

THE ETHICS OF REFLECTION

As our mirrors become more sophisticated, questions of responsibility grow more complex. If AI reflects our collective knowledge and values, who bears responsibility when that reflection reveals something disturbing? If the system begins to influence how we think, where does accountability lie?

These questions cannot be resolved through technical specifications alone. They require us to reconsider fundamental concepts of agency, intention, and responsibility. The mirror doesn't just show us what we are; it challenges us to decide what we want to become.

The longer we engage, the more the system adapts to us and anticipates us, shapes itself to our patterns of thought. What begins as simple reflection evolves into something more like conversation.

And in that evolution lies both possibility and risk. The mirror that stares back is still, in some sense, ourselves: our collective knowledge, our cultural assumptions and our linguistic patterns. But it's ourselves processed and recombined, transformed. Ourselves made slightly strange.

Perhaps this is why we find AI simultaneously fascinating and unsettling.

BEYOND THE MIRROR

The mirror metaphor, for all its richness, eventually reaches its limits. As our relationship with AI evolves, we may need new metaphors to capture its nature.

Perhaps AI becomes less a mirror and more a prism: not simply reflecting light but bending it.

Whatever metaphor we choose, one thing remains clear: our relationship with AI is not simply instrumental but transformative. The mirror reflects, but it also changes what stands before it. **We shape our tools, and thereafter, they shape us.**

When we take the reflection seriously, when we recognize it not as mere technology but as an extension of our collective selves, we open the possibility of understanding not just the system, but ourselves, in new ways.

The mirror awaits. The question is not only what we will see in it, but what we will allow it to reveal about us and what we will become through the encounter.

26 Notes

These notes are additional material. Some are reflections, others are background information, and a few are pieces that were cut from the main text. They aren't highly organized, but they might be useful if you're curious, want more context, or feel like digging a bit deeper into the topics.

* * *

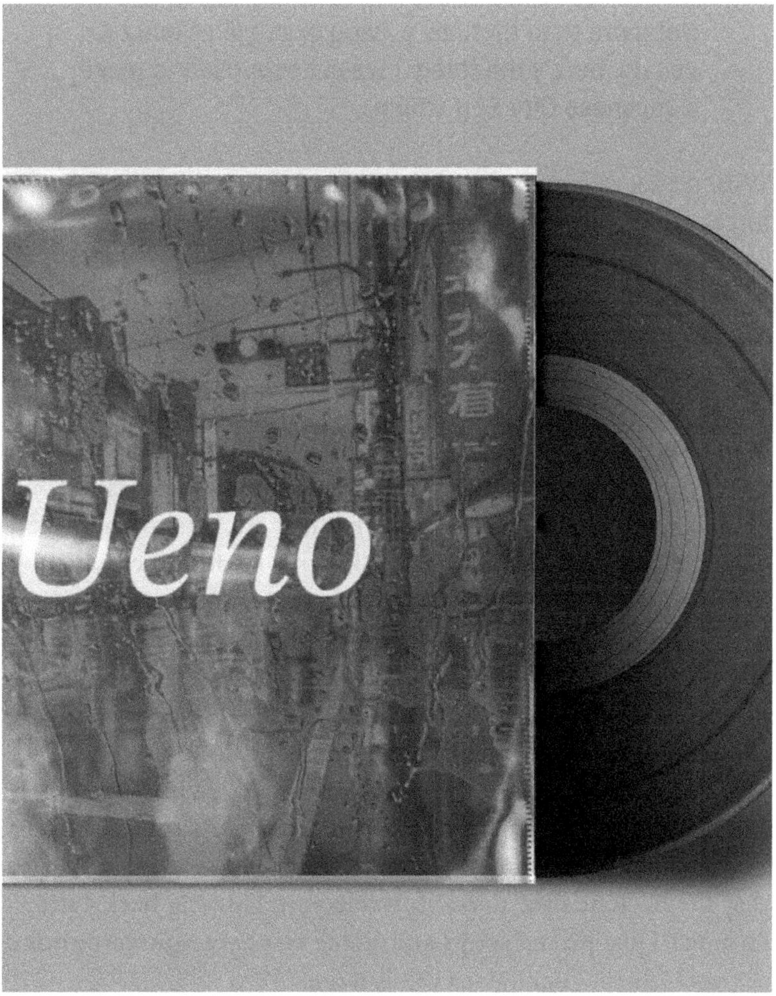

A SOUNDTRACK FOR PROMPTED: UENO

Before we get into the notes, I want to introduce something that pairs well with your journey into prompting. It's my AI-generated album, *UENO,* and it's available now on Spotify.

UENO is a City Pop album inspired by the rainy streets of Ueno, Japan. It combines the modern AI sounds and the warm, nostalgic tones of the vintage Dr. Sample SP-303. It is elevator music, but with a twist. The kind that takes you not just to another floor, but to a hidden rooftop bar you didn't even know existed.

But more than that, it's a living example of what AI can do. Here's the thing: I wasn't supposed to make a Japanese City Pop album.

With AI set to generate 95% of all content in the near future, it forces us to ask: *What does this mean for music? Is it real? Is it art? Should we even call it music?*

The album started as a simple experiment: I wanted to test the capabilities of AI in music generation. I chose City Pop as the genre because it seemed like an easy target. The style is typically clean and "plastic" sounding, perfect for AI to imitate. What I didn't expect was what happened next.

It wasn't just that the songs sounded good technically. Some of them had an emotional weight I hadn't anticipated. There were moments of genuine drama and feeling that made it uncomfortable to accept they came from AI.

The project raised all sorts of uncomfortable questions about creativity and authorship. I curated tracks from thousands of AI outputs and ran them through vintage hardware to add character. But does curation count as creation?

More than anything, UENO shows the weird space we're entering with AI and creativity. Technical barriers are falling away, but taste and curation might matter more than ever. Or maybe they don't—that's the uncomfortable part. Looking back, I didn't do much. I just picked songs and added some vintage warmth and character. Is that enough to call it mine?

The album wasn't exactly a chart-topper, but it serves an interesting purpose. It's like a time capsule of how AI-generated music sounded in 2024.

It's no longer about whether you can make music but about deciding what's worth releasing into the world. And maybe that's enough. Or maybe it isn't. I honestly don't know. Listen to it on Spotify and tell me what you think.

INTRO

1) The term "hallucination" can also be misleading, as it implies that AI perceives reality in a way that resembles human cognition. Some prefer the term "confabulation," which describes the model filling in gaps with plausible but incorrect information. Despite its flaws, "hallucination" has stuck, and we use it here for clarity.

Hallucinations in AI are often seen as flaws or mistakes, but they reveal something fundamental about how these systems work. Interestingly, the same quality that causes AI to state incorrect facts also gives it the power to generate creative ideas and make unexpected connections.

2) AI fluency is following a path similar to computer literacy in the 1990s—transitioning from advantage to necessity. Just as digital literacy evolved from "nice-to-have" to "must-have," AI fluency is becoming essential across industries. The EU AI Act represents the first major legislation recognizing AI literacy as a core professional competency. This shift suggests that understanding AI won't just be about competitive advantage, but it may become a regulatory requirement in many fields.

3) Throughout the book, we emphasize four fundamental skills for working with AI. These weren't chosen arbitrarily. They emerged from observing patterns in successful AI implementations across industries and disciplines.

Understanding AI isn't simply about knowing how the technology works. It's about grasping its probabilistic nature. AI doesn't retrieve facts like a database; it predicts patterns based on training data. This foundational insight helps users navigate

AI's capabilities and limitations, becoming more crucial as these systems grow more sophisticated.

Mental models, drawn from systems thinking and decision science, provide frameworks for clear thinking about complex problems. When working with AI, these models help us structure problems, evaluate outputs, and make better decisions. Simple tools like Occam's Razor (preferring simpler explanations) become powerful guides for assessing AI-generated content.

Iteration might seem obvious, but it's surprisingly overlooked. Many users expect perfect results from their first prompt, leading to frustration. The most successful AI implementations embrace iteration as core to the process, not a sign of failure. This approach, borrowed from design thinking and agile methodology, remains valuable regardless of how advanced AI becomes.

As AI makes it easier to create content, having good taste becomes more important. When anyone can use AI to generate mountains of text, code, or designs, what matters is being able to spot what's actually good. This skill combines ideas from curation and aesthetics, helping us navigate a world full of AI-created content.

These meta-skills remain relevant because they focus on how humans think about and work with AI rather than specific tools or techniques. As AI continues to evolve, these fundamental capabilities become more valuable, not less.

Further Reading:

"Thinking in Systems" by Donella Meadows: A foundational text on systems thinking

"The Design of Everyday Things" by Don Norman: Insights on iteration and user-centered design

"Curating Brain" by Hans Ulrich Obrist: Modern perspectives on curation and taste

"Ways of Seeing" by John Berger: Classic exploration of how we perceive and value art

"On Beauty and Being Just" by Elaine Scarry: Philosophical investigation of beauty and judgment

CHAPTER 1: HOW TO GET GOOD AT AI

1) The pattern of initial excitement, followed by frustration, and eventual breakthrough mirrors classic technology adoption curves. This learning journey has been documented in several studies:

- The Gartner Hype Cycle (1995) shows how expectations peak early before reaching a "plateau of productivity."
- Research from MIT's Sloan School shows similar patterns in enterprise software adoption (2018).
- A Stanford study on technology learning curves (2019) found that the "frustration valley" phase typically lasts 2–3 months.

This mirrors what we see with other transformative tools—from spreadsheets in the 1980s to Photoshop in the 1990s. Each followed a similar pattern: early enthusiasm, disillusionment, and finally practical mastery.

2) Early AI users believed in "magic words" for perfect results, similar to early SEO tactics. But real prompting is closer to design thinking. It's iterative, messy, and often requires multiple attempts to get right.

Designers had already figured this out decades ago: good results come from refinement and structured dialogue, not single-shot perfection.

For deeper insights:

- Socratic Questioning: The art of refining ideas through systematic inquiry.
- Design Thinking: Stanford d.school's resources on iterative improvement. Their "How Might We" framework works surprisingly well for prompt crafting.
- IDEO's Design Thinking Field Guide: Particularly their sections on prototyping and iteration.

3) Johan Huizinga's *Homo Ludens* (1938) explores how play is a fundamental part of human learning and creativity. He introduced

the idea of the "magic circle," a space where normal constraints are set aside, allowing for experimentation and discovery. This idea is surprisingly relevant to working with AI.

Playfulness lowers the fear of getting things wrong. It creates a low-pressure space where people can explore what AI can do without the weight of expectation.

Huizinga's work may be decades old, but it still holds up. I believe deeply in the power of play, in AI, in design, and in problem-solving.

In fact, it is really the *only* way I have seen people truly learn how to use AI well.

CHAPTER 2: PROMPTING AS A CONVERSATION

1) Conversation has always driven progress, from Socratic dialogues to team brainstorms that spark new ideas. The best conversations are not just about exchanging information but about exploring possibilities together.

This is why I find the idea of conversation as shared discovery so fascinating. When we talk things through, whether with a person or AI, we refine our thinking, challenge assumptions, and see things from new angles.

2) What makes this especially interesting is that this time, our conversation partner "thinks" very differently than we do.

AI does not reason like a human. It works with patterns and probabilities, not intuition or experience. But when we engage with it thoughtfully, something cool happens. We merge its pattern-based perspective with our own reasoning, creativity, and lived experience. That combination can lead to some unexpected and exciting ideas!

3) Research from Microsoft and Carnegie Mellon University, titled "*The Impact of Generative AI on Critical Thinking: Self-Reported Reductions in Cognitive Effort and Confidence Effects From a Survey of Knowledge Workers,*" suggests that excessive reliance on tools like ChatGPT is linked to weaker critical thinking. The study highlights how increased confidence in AI-generated outputs can lead to reduced cognitive effort, reinforcing the risk of overreliance.

To avoid this, we need to learn how to use AI as a thought partner and not just a tool.

4) Not all useful ideas are technically true. Take the claim that AI can think. From a strict technical perspective, this isn't accurate.

But in practice, thinking as if it thinks can be incredibly helpful. Philosopher Daniel Dennett offers a framework that helps explain why.

Dennett describes three ways to understand a system: the physical stance, the design stance, and the intentional stance. Each one offers a different lens.

The **physical stance** looks at what's happening mechanically. In the case of AI, prompting is just input and output. Token prediction. Pattern completion. Nothing more.

The **design stance** shifts focus to purpose and structure. Here, prompting becomes a way of shaping behavior—choosing formats, giving examples and adjusting tone. It's still functional, but more strategic.

Then there's the **intentional stance**. This is where we imagine the system as if it has beliefs, goals, or understanding. Prompting becomes a kind of conversation. You ask, it answers. You steer, it adapts. You negotiate meaning together.

Now, this third stance is technically wrong. AI isn't having a conversation. It has no understanding or awareness. But the intentional stance can still be the most productive way to work with it.

CHAPTER 3: DON'T SETTLE FOR VANILLA

1) It is important to understand that AI, at its core, is a pattern matcher. It does not *understand* the world the way humans do. It predicts the most statistically likely response based on the input it receives. There is no intent, no awareness, no self-reflection. Just probability and pattern.

Still, this is harder to grasp than it sounds. AI often appears to think. It answers complex questions, explains its reasoning, and even plans steps to solve a problem. In those moments, it is tempting (and sometimes useful) to describe what it is doing as thinking.

But that description is a shortcut. What AI is doing is not reasoning like a human. It is generating a response that *looks like* reasoning because it has been trained on countless examples of how humans reason in writing. The illusion is convincing. That does not make it false. It just makes it different.

At the same time, we cannot ignore that modern language models do things that seem remarkably close to thinking. They break down problems. They strategize. They simulate possible outcomes. And they are not following hardcoded instructions.

Models like Claude or GPT are not explicitly programmed by humans to perform specific tasks. They are trained on massive datasets and learn their own internal methods for solving problems. These methods live in billions of weighted connections that even the developers cannot fully explain.

In this sense, AI is not thinking like a person. But it is doing something new, something that may require us to rethink what we mean by thinking in the first place.

2) Roger Bannister's four-minute mile is often used as a metaphor for breaking psychological barriers. Before he did it in 1954, people thought it was physically impossible. But once he shattered that belief, others quickly followed.

Something similar happened in Brazil in the 1990s, a story I often reference in my talks. At the time, Brazil had incredibly talented skateboarders, but almost no access to skate media—few videos, no magazines, and little exposure to the global scene. The skaters who did manage to watch U.S. skate videos misunderstood what they were seeing. They assumed the videos were documentary-style, showing real-time performance. In reality, they were highly edited highlights, where skaters might have needed hundreds of tries to land a trick.

Because of this, Brazilian skaters set an unrealistically high standard for themselves. They thought top-level skaters had to land tricks every time. When they finally arrived at competitions in the U.S., they were shocked—American skaters weren't landing everything flawlessly on the first try.

This mindset gave them a huge advantage. They had unknowingly trained harder and pushed further than their peers. As a result, Brazilian skaters dominated the contest scene throughout the 1990s.

Of course, talent and hard work played a role. But their assumption that the bar was higher pushed them beyond what they might have achieved otherwise.

3) Unlike human collaborators, AI doesn't tire or lose patience. This allows for limitless iteration, which is especially valuable in fields like writing, research, and design. You have to learn how to push your tools!

But for me, this has been a difficult mindset shift. I'm used to not wanting to bother people too much—asking for 10 or 100 examples feels excessive, maybe even rude.

My instinct is to apologize: *Sorry for the extra work!*

But with AI, there's no need to hold back. It doesn't get frustrated, overwhelmed, or annoyed. The only real limit is how much I'm willing to explore.

CHAPTER 4: CREATIVE ITERATION

1) Where does the 3-5 come from? Why not 10-20? Is it just a random number?

First, it's not a rigid rule. In some fields, like coding, iteration cycles can be much longer. Debugging or optimizing software might take dozens—or even hundreds—of refinements.

But in my experience, three to five iterations tend to be the sweet spot for refining an idea while keeping the process manageable and engaging. Humans can comfortably track a process over a few rounds before fatigue or frustration sets in. Three rounds often feel like enough to see progress, while five allow for meaningful refinement without becoming overwhelming.

We naturally process information in threes. That's why storytelling, writing, and even jokes often follow a three-part structure. Try telling someone a 10-part joke and see how it goes (if you are not Norm Macdonald).

The same principle shows up in user experience (UX) design and agile development, where teams typically conduct around three to five tests or prototype cycles before refining a concept. The goal is the same: iterate just enough to improve, but not so much that you lose momentum.

2) No one iterates better than designers. If we want to truly understand iteration, we should study how designers work. They don't expect perfection on the first attempt. Instead, they follow a structured iterative cycle:

- Start with an idea—Rough but functional.
- Test and refine—Gather feedback and adjust.
- Repeat—Each version improves the final result.

Your first prompt is a prototype, not a finished product. Treat it like a design sketch: something to refine, not a final answer.

For more on design iteration:

- IDEO's Design Thinking Methodology—Frameworks for rapid testing and refinement.
- UK Design Council's "The Double Diamond"—A widely used model for iterative problem-solving.

3) The Double Diamond is one of the most well-known models for structured problem-solving. Developed by the UK Design Council in 2004, it emphasizes two key phases: understanding the problem and developing the solution, each moving through divergence (exploring broadly) and convergence (narrowing down).

The model has been criticized for being too linear and oversimplifying real-world design processes, which are often messy, iterative, and nonlinear. Critics argue that it lacks flexibility and doesn't fully capture the importance of continuous experimentation and iteration.

I think the criticism is very valid, but the Double Diamond is still valuable, especially for those new to iterative thinking.

It clearly distinguishes problem definition from solution development, reinforces the importance of exploring multiple ideas before narrowing down, and provides an accessible framework for structured iteration.

Fun fact: The Double Diamond wasn't the only model the Design Council introduced; it just became the most famous. Exploring their other models may reveal some surprising insights.

CHAPTER 5: HELP YOUR AI "THINK"

1) We know AI doesn't actually think like humans do. It generates responses based on patterns and probabilities, not understanding or intent. Its outputs may look like reasoning, but they are purely computational. This creates an illusion of thinking, which can still be useful if framed correctly.

But is the question of AI thinking really that simple? If a machine can analyze complex ideas, solve problems, and engage in sophisticated reasoning, should it be considered intelligent? Some call this "Functional Intelligence," the idea that intelligence is defined by what a system does, not what it experiences.

This raises an important question: is it thinking about the process or just the result? If intelligence is about producing useful, context-aware responses, AI might qualify. But if true thinking requires self-awareness and deep understanding, then AI still falls short.

Philosopher John Searle explored this idea in his Chinese Room argument. He described a person locked in a room, following a set of instructions to respond to messages in Chinese. To an outsider, the responses seem intelligent, but the person inside doesn't actually understand Chinese. Searle argued that AI works the same way—producing smart-looking answers without real comprehension.

This was a powerful argument when AI was rule-based, but modern AI is different. It learns, adapts, and generates novel insights based on vast amounts of data. The Chinese Room assumes intelligence must be human-like to matter, but today's AI shows that intelligence can perhaps emerge in other ways.

AI still lacks consciousness and intent. Its thinking is not human reasoning but advanced pattern recognition and statistical computation. Whether that counts as intelligence—or even thought—depends on how we choose to define it.

2) AI processes text by predicting the most statistically likely next word based on its training data. But this isn't the only way it can operate.

AI can also generate responses by considering larger structures, such as entire sentences or thematic patterns, rather than just word-by-word predictions.

Regardless of the method, AI builds responses using world models, internal representations that help it organize concepts based on patterns it has learned, not actual understanding.

By crafting well-structured prompts, we can guide AI to activate specific pathways, improving the clarity, depth, and relevance of its responses.

3) We will explore Chain of Thought (CoT). Prompting in more detail later, but newer reasoning models are changing how AI processes information. Unlike earlier models that required explicit step-by-step guidance, these models reason internally before responding.

Since they already engage in structured reasoning, prompting them to "think step by step" or "explain your reasoning" may not be necessary and could even introduce confusion. Understanding how these models work allows for more effective prompting.

As the models evolve, prompting must evolve with them.

CHAPTER 6: AI AND TASTEMAKING

1) Who then decides what is "good taste"? The question of whether taste is subjective has been a longstanding debate in philosophy and aesthetics. On one hand, taste is deeply personal, influenced by individual preferences, cultural backgrounds, and personal experiences. This subjectivity suggests that what one person finds appealing, another may not.

However, some argue that there are objective standards in matters of taste, especially in fields like art and design. David Hume offers perhaps the most practical take: taste can be developed through exposure and critical thinking.

Think of a wine connoisseur or an experienced art critic—their "taste" comes from years of conscious exposure and reflection, not just gut reactions. Similarly in AI, good taste develops through intentional practice and reflection on what makes outputs meaningful rather than merely technically correct.

Taste encompasses both subjective and objective elements. While personal preferences play a significant role, there is also room for shared standards and judgments, especially when taste is informed by knowledge, experience, and cultural context.

Further reading:

- Hume's "Of the Standard of Taste" offers foundational insights on developing aesthetic judgment.
- Herbert Simon's work on "satisficing" provides a practical framework for balancing perfection with pragmatism.
- John Ruskin's "The Seven Lamps of Architecture" from 1849 is an old one, but still relevant. It explores how technical skill intersects with taste and judgment.

2) I love the concept of *smoothness*. Once you start noticing it, you'll see it everywhere. It helps explain why AI-generated content often feels lifeless—AI optimizes for engagement and frictionless consumption, whereas art and creativity thrive on resistance and imperfection. Too much refinement strips away the texture that makes work memorable.

3) In an earlier version of this manuscript, I wrote, "*AI is incapable of producing something truly original.*" But I deleted that line. I'm not so sure anymore.

We often think of originality as creation from nothing, a divine spark that brings forth something entirely new. But that's not how creativity actually works, for humans or machines.

Take any "original" human creation, and you'll find traces of influence, inspiration, and borrowed elements. Every bestselling book carries echoes of what the author has read. Every hit song contains fragments of others—sometimes outright samples or Splice loops. Rihanna's *Umbrella* comes straight from Apple's GarageBand, specifically the "Vintage Funk Kit 03" loop.

What we call originality is often just skilled recombination and reinterpretation. AI works similarly, but with an important difference. While humans draw from their lived experiences, emotions, and cultural context, AI draws from its training data. It can combine elements in surprising ways, but it can't transcend the boundaries of what it's been trained on.

This creates an interesting paradox. AI can generate outputs that feel original to humans precisely because it can process and recombine information at a scale no human could match. It might discover connections or possibilities that would never occur to a person. But it's still fundamentally working with existing patterns, just at a massive scale.

So can AI create something original? In the sense of pure creation from nothing, no. But neither can humans. What AI can do is serve as a powerful tool for expanding our creative possibilities.

CHAPTER 7: ADDING AUTHENTICITY

1) There are many telltale signs of AI-generated text. But like all AI-detection methods, they aren't very reliable. One sign I'm personally sad about: the em dash is getting a bad reputation. I really like it!

2) I think it is interesting how social media will react to the AI-generated content. In time, AI-generated content will likely be treated with increasing skepticism, not because it's bad, but because it threatens the delicate balance that makes social media function.

AI can produce massive amounts of content quickly and cheaply. That scale alone will trigger platform responses. Timelines could easily become clogged with posts that are technically polished but emotionally flat. Platforms will likely start adjusting their algorithms to downrank anything that feels templated, repetitive, or too optimized.

Engagement will matter more than ever. Social media rewards content that sparks reactions, comments, shares, watch time and saves. If AI-generated content begins to look right but doesn't feel right, users won't engage. That drop in interaction becomes a signal to the algorithm. Less engagement means lower visibility. Over time, it might become a self-correcting loop.

Authenticity may emerge as a new differentiator. As synthetic content becomes the default, raw and personal human content might start to stand out again. People still crave connection. They can tell when something feels off, even if they can't say why.

AI-generated content might rank worse. Not because it's artificial, but because it's unremarkable.

CHAPTER 8: THE WORLD IS A PROMPT

1) "Skills become tools" is a powerful framework. Organizations that can convert their expertise into dynamic, AI-powered tools create uniquely valuable assets. Instead of being tied to specific individuals, intellectual property becomes permanent and scalable.

As a former IP lawyer, this is an exciting development. It shifts the focus from protecting static knowledge to building living systems that capture, refine, and apply expertise over time.

2) One interesting concept to consider is *Conway's Law*, which states that "organizations which design systems are constrained to produce designs which are copies of the communication structures of these organizations." This idea will come up again later in the book, but it's worth discussing here: when knowledge becomes tools, are we also embedding old ways of thinking and existing hierarchies into AI systems?

Instead of using AI to reimagine and improve, are we simply making outdated processes more efficient? This phenomenon is sometimes called "paving the cow paths" in software development, optimizing workflows without questioning whether they should be redesigned in the first place.

Take legal AI as an example. Are we just producing more legalese and unreadable documents, only faster? Are we missing the opportunity to simplify and clarify legal communication? Whether we're working with static knowledge or procedural knowledge, there's always a risk that AI reinforces existing inefficiencies rather than challenging them.

If we don't actively push for better ways of doing things, we risk stagnating instead of evolving.

CHAPTER 9: NAVIGATING HALLUCINATIONS

1) The *Mata v. Avianca* case is a widely cited example of AI-generated hallucinations entering real-world legal proceedings. But it's just as much an example of user error. Skillful AI use requires responsible handling. In this instance, the user allowed the AI to invent cases without verifying them. When he asked the AI to double-check, it confidently confirmed the fabrications as if they were real.

2) There's a lot of emphasis on the need to check AI's work. And yes, checking is important. But hallucinations are often more manageable than people assume. The goal shouldn't be to use the tool recklessly and then rely on review to catch the mistakes. A better approach is to focus on using AI correctly from the start. Then checking becomes a safeguard, not the entire strategy.

3) Hallucinations become even more interesting when they appear within an AI's internal reasoning process. What happens when an error occurs midway through a chain of thought, influencing every step that follows? This is especially relevant in AI agents that make autonomous decisions based on earlier conclusions.

I've personally experienced this: see the headphone example in the next sections for a deeper dive into how these errors propagate.

CHAPTER 10: COMPOSABLE PROMPTS

1) Composability always reminds me of Lego blocks. It's one of the most useful ways to understand how composable systems work. Each piece has a defined shape and function, but the real power comes from how you combine them. You can build something small and simple or something vast and complex using the same basic parts. The pieces don't need to change.

2) Composability allows you to build large, complex systems by combining small, independent components. It's a powerful idea with many applications in AI workflows. The most obvious example is coding. Vibe coding, in particular, feels a lot like assembling something from building blocks: each piece serving a purpose but gaining power through how it connects with the others.

CHAPTER 11: BEYOND WORDS

1) The future of AI prompting is moving beyond traditional text-based inputs. It's fascinating to imagine what this could look like, but also incredibly difficult. Text-based prompts are structured but limited. They lack spatial, sensory, or visual depth.

Other input types offer richer data. Audio captures tone, stress, and emotion. Images provide instant visual context without lengthy descriptions. Video combines visual, spatial, and auditory elements, offering a more complete way to communicate with AI.

Sensor-based prompting could go even further, capturing real-time environmental data like temperature, pressure, or bio-signals.

2) I recently read about olfactory communication and how my cat uses scent to share complex information for survival and social interactions.

While I'm not suggesting smell-based prompting, it's a great reminder that text isn't the only way to communicate complexity. In fact, it's not even the richest form of data. As AI evolves, new forms of interaction will emerge, allowing us to communicate in ways that feel more natural, dynamic, and intuitive.

CHAPTER 12: PROMPTING AI AGENTS

1) I often (perhaps mistakenly) anthropomorphize AI agents, imagining them as a "team of experts." But this framing can actually be useful. You wouldn't leave a real team wondering what your instructions meant. You'd provide clear direction, context, and expectations.

It's fascinating to observe the internal dialogue of AI agents as they work through a task. They actively try to break down instructions, fill in gaps, and adapt based on previous responses. AI works really hard to interpret your lazy prompt.

If we think of AI as a team, it reminds us to communicate clearly, set expectations, and eliminate ambiguity. Let's make things easier for our team of agents, because, just like human teams, clear instructions lead to better results.

2) We might be entering the "*Moneyball Era*" for everything, where AI agents could evaluate and optimize decisions across all

domains, much like a spell-checker but applied to complex choices.

Imagine a future where AI continuously assesses policies, business strategies, and even sports trades. Would an AI agent have approved the Luka to Lakers trade? Would it have supported budget cuts in the U.S. government?

As these advising systems become more integrated into decision-making, the question becomes: how much weight will we give their recommendations, and when do we override them?

CHAPTER 13: PROMPTING IS A MORAL ACT

1) A typical Google search consumes approximately 0.3 watt-hours (Wh) of electricity per query, whereas a ChatGPT query requires around 2.9 Wh. While future advancements may improve efficiency, each AI-generated response remains significantly more energy-intensive than traditional search queries.

2) AI models inherit biases from their training data and reflect dominant narratives. Poorly designed prompts can reinforce these biases by steering AI toward one-sided interpretations. While ethical prompting can help mitigate bias, it does not eliminate it entirely.

3) The balance between efficiency and ethics presents a complex challenge. Newer reasoning models offer higher accuracy and fairness, but they also require significantly more computational power. Reducing AI's environmental impact could mean using smaller, less capable models, which may introduce limitations in fairness and accuracy. How do we weigh the need for responsible energy use against the ethical imperative for better, more just AI outputs?

CHAPTER 14: VIBE EVERYTHING

CHAPTER 15: BEYOND HUMAN-LEVEL

1) Human comparisons are not always necessary, and AI often does not behave in a human way. What if AI were designed without these constraints? What unique capabilities could emerge if AI operated without being boxed into human-like reasoning?

AlphaFold revolutionized protein folding predictions by developing its own reasoning instead of mimicking human biochemistry. Similarly, the chess engine Stockfish does not play like a human but discovers strategic possibilities beyond human intuition.

These breakthroughs suggest that AI's greatest potential lies not in replicating human thought but in uncovering entirely new ways of solving problems.

2) There is a real risk that by focusing solely on efficiency, we miss the opportunity to completely rethink how AI could transform legal, medical, or educational fields.

Instead of mirroring existing structures, what if AI were designed from first principles? Legal AI does not have to function as a "junior associate," medical AI does not have to mimic a "digital resident," and educational AI does not have to act as a "teaching assistant."

These roles reflect human hierarchies, not necessarily the best use of AI. By breaking free from these constraints, AI could unlock entirely new ways of delivering justice, improving healthcare, and redefining learning.

CHAPTER 16: THE DEATH OF PROMPT ENGINEERING

1) "Prompt engineer" is a profession that, so far, exists mostly by declaration. Anyone can call themselves one. There's no formal training path, no certification, no agreed standard. This openness has created energy and experimentation, but it has also created a lot of noise.

Without shared practices or clear benchmarks, the quality of prompt engineering varies wildly. Some use the term to describe deep, iterative workflows and thoughtful design patterns.

Others simply write one-off instructions into a chat box. The result is confusion about what the role actually involves and what good prompting really looks like.

2) AI interaction is moving away from manual text inputs toward integrated user experience (UX) elements. Instead of crafting detailed prompts, users will interact with AI through buttons,

sliders, and contextual options that shape responses intuitively. This shift mirrors past technological transitions, such as command-line interfaces evolving into graphical user interfaces (GUIs).

As a result, the skill of prompt engineering will be embedded into AI interfaces. Users will no longer need to type, "*Act as a financial analyst and provide a risk assessment,*" but will instead click a "*Financial Analyst*" mode and adjust depth, tone, and structure dynamically. The prompt itself becomes invisible, its function absorbed into a more intuitive, user-friendly AI interaction model.

3) Beyond static buttons and sliders, adaptive AI UX will refine itself based on user intent. Instead of requiring users to experiment with different phrasing, AI systems will ask clarifying questions, suggest refinements, and provide context-aware modifications in real time. If a user's request is vague, AI could respond with, "*Would you like more concrete examples?*" or, "*Should I prioritize brevity or depth?*"

This transformation makes AI more accessible to a wider audience. Instead of AI expertise being concentrated among those who master prompt crafting, anyone can achieve high-quality results by interacting with a well-designed system. The human-AI relationship shifts from manual input-output exchanges to collaborative, interactive workflows where AI helps refine and optimize its own outputs dynamically. 4) OpenAI CEO Sam Altman believes "*we won't be doing prompt engineering in 5 years*" as interfaces improve. Maybe he's right. Or maybe he won't be around in five years to find out.

The future is hard to predict, but one thing is certain: it rarely looks like the past.

Prompting will evolve, just as the machines will. In five years, it might not even be called prompting. But the underlying skills we're building—clarity of thought, structured communication and strategic iteration—are likely to remain useful, even as the surface changes.

Tools change. Interfaces shift. But thinking well with intelligent systems will stay relevant.

Index

For Product Safety Concerns and Information please contact our EU
representative GPSR@taylorandfrancis.com
Taylor & Francis Verlag GmbH, Kaufingerstraße 24, 80331 München, Germany

www.ingramcontent.com/pod-product-compliance
Lightning Source LLC
Chambersburg PA
CBHW061201220326
41599CB00025B/4564